Solutions for Business, Culture and Religion in Eastern Europe and Beyond

Sebastian Văduva • Ioan Ş. Fotea
Andrew R. Thomas
Editors

Solutions for Business, Culture and Religion in Eastern Europe and Beyond

The 2016 Griffiths School of Management Annual Conference on Business, Entrepreneurship and Ethics (GSMAC)

Springer

UNIVERSITATEA EMANUEL DIN ORADEA

Editors
Sebastian Văduva
Griffiths School of Management
Emanuel University of Oradea
Oradea, Romania

Ioan Ş. Fotea
Griffiths School of Management
Emanuel University of Oradea
Oradea, Romania

Andrew R. Thomas
Marketing and International Business
University of Akron
Broadview Heights, OH, USA

ISBN 978-3-319-63368-8 ISBN 978-3-319-63369-5 (eBook)
DOI 10.1007/978-3-319-63369-5

Library of Congress Control Number: 2017952605

Printed on acid-free paper

This Springer imprint is published by Springer Nature
The registered company is Springer International Publishing AG
The registered company address is: Gewerbestrasse 11, 6330 Cham, Switzerland

Preface

The papers in this book were discussed and disseminated at the 7th Annual Griffiths School of Management International Conference on Business and Ethics, organized by Emanuel University of Oradea in May 2016. The conference provided a platform for academics and practitioners in the fields of business and leadership to interact and debate on the different dimensions of ethics in business and leadership in the context of developing, growing, and financing Romanian organizations, both public and private.

During the transitional phase from communism to democracy that many countries from Central and Eastern Europe faced, there was an increased consideration regarding the impact that this transition would have on poverty. The author of the article "Improving Socioeconomic Opportunities for the Poor: A Study of Poverty Measurement in Romania" provides valuable information and uses data in order to provide poverty measures, while also highlighting the most important studies published on this subject.

"An Empirical Analysis of Herzberg's Two-Factor od Work Motivation Applied on Hospital Employees in Jordan" analyzes the factors that motivate employees to strive toward a better job performance. The authors apply the Two-Factor Theory of Herzberg on a sample of 325 employees from 6 hospitals in Jordan, in order to find out which aspects from both the hygiene and the growth motivation factors are the most sought after by the hospital workers. The findings, even though applied to hospital employees, are illustrative of the values placed by workers in any field.

The efficiency of an organization can be greatly increased by an ongoing assessment of its employees. Oftentimes, this process is overlooked, causing numerous problems within the organization. This assessment is especially important in the medical sector, where the personnel face many challenges. The author of the article "Assessment of Employments: An Essential Process in Increasing the Efficiency of Human Capital Use Within the Romanian Health-Care Facilities" provides a study based on three representative hospitals in Romania and gives insight regarding employment issues that Romanian medical personnel are faced with. The study argues that periodical assessment of employments would radically improve the efficiency of medical facilities and it would also increase employee satisfaction by providing a healthy communication that would enable positive changes.

The authors of "The Impact of Cross-Border Cooperation on Human Resources Employed in Local Administration: The Case of the Romanian-Hungarian Border Area" present a survey-based research that aims to identify the main issues pertaining to human resources in local administration and the key objectives that managers and project leaders need to undertake in order to efficiently fulfill the projects pertaining to cross-border cooperation.

"Am I Able to Be an Entrepreneur?" is the title of a research that aims to answer a very pertinent question on whether we are born or formed as entrepreneurs. The author gives insight into fields such as genetic, neurobiology, and psychology, thus providing an interdisciplinary view on this topic. Even though research highlights that entrepreneurial behavior is determined by genes and early childhood, this article argues that entrepreneurial training and education has a big impact on the ability to think and act like an entrepreneur.

The authors in Chap. 6 propose a solution to increasing sales by approaching this area from a multi- and interdisciplinary point of view. "Scientific Selling: Improving Sales Performance Through Applied Psychology. Case Study on a Romanian Company" highlights the importance of knowing and recognizing the different types of personalities and clothing tendencies that people have, in order to better serve clients and in order to increase sales. The theoretical data gleaned by the authors was used for an experiment on a Romanian company, thus analyzing the complex world of client/consumer behavior and its impact on sales.

The importance of mentoring and guiding novice teacher is a subject debated in the article "The Need for Mentoring in the Preuniversity Educational System." The current state of education is a topic that has caused numerous discussions and debates, the underlying conclusion being the need for reform and improvement. This research shows that a mentoring program that provides sufficient support to new teachers would greatly enhance the quality of the educational system.

Most companies wish for a higher degree of product quality and economic increase, but not all are ready to invest in human resources. The author of the research paper "Recruitment and Selection of Human Resources in the Romanian Organizations" argues the importance of motivating employees and highlights the direct correlation between the quality of people hired and the increase in economic activity.

"Identifying the Main Factors of Workplace Flexibility Among Romanian Employees" is a research that demonstrates the importance of offering employees the opportunity to choose elements of workforce flexibility. The study includes a case study that encompasses the opinions of 100 Romanian employees, and the results show that the most important factors cited were autonomy of work teams and work time flexibility.

Obtaining profit is one of the main purposes of an entrepreneur, but the way that this profit is spent and reinvested is just as important. "Compounding in Romania" is a research paper that argues the positive effects that reinvesting profit can have on the prosperity of a business, with a specific analysis on the situation in Romania.

Religion is a subject that has caused numerous debates and conflicts throughout time. The article "How Religion Influences Economic Development: A Case on Romania" argues that a correlation between the prosperity of different counties in Romania and the values of the most important Christian denominations exists, thus demonstrating the influence that these denominations have on economic prosperity. This research includes a case study on Romania, in which GDP per capita, unemployment rate, average net wage, and poverty are analyzed in relationship to the Christian denominations.

The article "The Compatibility Between the Music Expectations of Church Leaders and the Training of Church Musicians in Romania: A Case Study" gives insight into the problems that arise when a disconnect between the needs of an employer and the skill sets of potential employees exists. This issue can also be found in the religious music sector, where the church leader oftentimes has a set of expectations, which are not met by the church musician. The authors of this research used two survey instruments to reveal the most important issues that pertain to the compatibility between the church as a possible employer of church musicians and the music graduates, as potential church music employees.

We trust that you will find this useful.

Oradea, Romania — Sebastian Văduva
Oradea, Romania — Ioan Ş. Fotea
Broadview Heights, OH, USA — Andrew R. Thomas

Contents

Chapter 1
Improving Socioeconomic Opportunities for the Poor: A Study of Poverty Measurement in Romania

Sorin Dan

Abstract This chapter estimates the extent and trend of poverty in Romania during transition, using grouped distributional data and Lorenz curve interpolation. It asks the question: do estimates derived from grouped distributional data differ from those in the literature derived from survey data? It finds that the poverty estimates introduced in this chapter are only broadly in line with the literature for the period 2002–2005 and document a substantial decline in poverty. The estimates for the late 1990s suggest that poverty in Romania fluctuated considerably during this period, which reflects the trend estimated in part of the literature. However, there are significant differences in the size of the estimated measures. This is also the case between estimates found in the literature derived from survey data. The chapter concludes by discussing the broader implications of using grouped distributional data and Lorenz curve interpolation in poverty research in Romania and elsewhere.

Keywords Poverty • Estimation • Grouped data • POVCAL • Romania

1.1 Introduction

The measurement and analysis of poverty in the former communist countries in Central and Eastern Europe (CEE) have received increasing attention during the transition from communism to democracy and market economy. Most of these countries have become members of the European Union (in the 2003 and 2007 accession waves, and Croatia in 2013)—a turning point marking the departure from a long-standing label of a transition state to a functional democracy and market economy. Although these societies have undergone a tremendous transformation in the 20-year transition and Europeanization period, much is still to be accomplished to respond to the increasing expectations of the citizens in the region.

S. Dan (✉)
Griffiths School of Management, Emanuel University of Oradea, Oradea, Romania
e-mail: sorin.dan@emanuel.ro

S. Văduva et al. (eds.), *Solutions for Business, Culture and Religion in Eastern Europe and Beyond*, DOI 10.1007/978-3-319-63369-5_1

The measurement of poverty in the new EU member states has experienced change as new data and methodological tools have become increasingly available. National statistical offices have harmonized their procedures in accordance with the EU *Acquis Communautaire* and are collaborating with Eurostat, the statistical office of the EU. International research expertise has likewise had an impact on the development of poverty measurement and estimation techniques. The World Bank country offices have provided much of this expertise.

This chapter looks at the estimation of poverty in Romania during transition. By transition we mean the period prior to the accession to the EU on January 1, 2007. It first compares studies from the literature to understand the similarities and differences in data, estimation methods, and the estimates obtained. It then argues that new estimates are needed and provides a set of poverty estimates using grouped (or aggregated) distributional data and compares them to alternative sets from earlier studies. We ask the following empirical question: do poverty estimates derived on the basis of grouped distributional data differ from those in the literature based on survey data?

This case study of Romanian poverty has broader implications for poverty measurement globally. Grouped data have been widely used in global poverty assessments mostly, but not exclusively, when unit record data are not available to estimate long-term poverty trends (e.g., Minoiu & Reddy, 2008a). Reasons for using grouped data include efficiency in processing the data and lack of availability to researchers of unit record data, which, unlike grouped data, are typically not included in public records. Moreover, the use of grouped data with an appropriate estimation method such as Lorenz curve interpolation has been used in the literature as a shortcut when estimates are needed for an auxiliary analysis or in a cross-country study. In this chapter, we estimate poverty over a longer term than measured in the literature, and this way, we seek to contribute to existing work on the subject of Romanian poverty. The uses of grouped data and Lorenz curve interpolation as applied to the Romanian case have broader implications for poverty research in other countries, where unit record data are not publicly available. To our knowledge, this method has not yet been used to estimate poverty or inequality in the country. In conclusion to their assessment of this method, Minoiu and Reddy (2008a, p. 8) argued: "Since grouped data will continue to be an important source of information – and often the only one – in poverty and inequality analysis, future research should aim to more fully establish the relative empirical performance of these alternatives and to develop new methods." We follow this argument and seek to investigate how estimates obtained with this method differ from those estimated on the basis of other alternative methods, found in Romanian data. For this reason, this chapter allocates significant space to first describe and compare existing estimates and then, second, to compare the estimates introduced in this chapter with existing ones.

The rest of the chapter is organized as follows. In Sects. 1.2 and 1.3, we review the poverty estimation literature in Romania. In Sect. 1.4 we introduce the methodology, followed by a description of the data. The results are presented in Sect. 1.5. Section 1.6 concludes and discusses implications for research on poverty on a more general level.

1.2 Poverty in Romania

Research on poverty in the former communist countries began to take shape in the early 1990s once these countries embarked on the road from communism to democracy and market economy. This transformation was known to be associated with an increase in poverty and inequality due to inherent downturns in economic output and the insufficient resources for social spending needed to compensate for the effects of structural transformation (Milanovic, 1998; World Bank, 1997).

Romania is a particularly interesting case for research on poverty due to the relative size of the country, the depth of the problems, and legacy inherited from the communist era. Various commentators have argued that communism in Romania, unlike in many other countries in the region, was communism "gone mad." The focus of the communist regime on heavy industry to fuel economic growth triggered increasing foreign debt following the oil crisis of 1979. To pay the foreign debt, the regime imposed a system of economic autarky in the 1980s, which ultimately eliminated the debt, but led to increasing poverty and discontent among the population (e.g., Molnar, 2000). Although a problem in the entire region, poverty was particularly extreme in Romania during transition. Following the collapse of communism in December 1989, a major factor associated with poverty was the sharp decline in economic output in the late 1990s, which were marked by two financial crises. Economic growth only resumed to a more sustained path in the early 2000s and came to a halt with the global financial crisis of 2008–2009.

The World Bank regional and national offices were the ones that mainly conducted research on poverty measurement during transition, in the form of broad poverty assessments. For this reason we first analyze comparatively the research headed by the World Bank. The main reason for focusing on World Bank studies is that during the transition period, the World Bank had a significant influence on shaping research practices on poverty measurement in the country.

The World Bank's work on the topic includes a comprehensive report on poverty and social policy in the early transition stage. This report estimated that the poverty headcount index (defined as the percentage of poor individuals in the total population) in 1994 was 21.52%, the poverty gap index (capturing the depth of poverty) was 5.50%, and the squared poverty gap index (denoting the severity of poverty) was 2.12% (World Bank, 1997). These standard poverty measures were based on a national poverty line of $3.30/day per capita (in constant international USD and April 1994 prices). The report used survey data from the Family Budget Survey[1] and Romanian Integrated Household Survey[2] and found that the increasing

[1] The Family Budget Survey (FBS), in Romanian Ancheta bugetelor de familie, implemented during 1989–1993, was not nationally representative and suffered from major sampling errors. The survey was based on a sample population of whom 71% resided in wage-earning households while the 1992 census showed that only 59% of individuals resided in such households (World Bank, 1997, Volume 2, Annex 1, p. 6).

[2] The Romanian Integrated Household Survey (RIHS) or in Romanian Ancheta integrată în gospodării (AIG) was a nationally representative household survey implemented in Romania since March 1994.

trend in poverty was due primarily to a sharp decline in economic output (i.e., changes in the mean of the income distribution) as opposed to changes in inequality (the shape of the distribution). The report concluded that poverty in Romania was deep—the average income of the poor was estimated to be 26% below the poverty line.

Another study conducted in the first half of the 1990s focused on the distributive impact of public social assistance programs using survey data from the 1994 RIHS (Subbarao & Mehra, 1995). The study found that social transfers helped reduce the incidence and depth of poverty but a large share of the poor population did not benefit from social transfers, and better targeting could have led to significant gains in poverty reduction.

Since different studies on poverty measurement employed different methodological approaches, comparison is problematic. However, this is not the only potential problem in estimating poverty identified in the literature. Poverty estimates in a transition context can be affected by survey design errors (e.g., Milanovic, 1998). For instance, surveys can be representative of certain social groups but not representative at the national level. In the case of the former communist countries, this reflected a Marxist view of society composed of social classes (Milanovic, 1998). The data collected by the FBS in the early 1990s in Romania, for instance, was only representative of the wage-earning households and not of the national population (World Bank, 1997).

1.3 Estimating Poverty in Romania During Transition: A Detailed Look at Two Studies

This section looks in greater detail at two studies, which measured poverty in transitional Romania, namely, Teşliuc, Pop, and Panduru (2003) and Alam et al. (2005). To our knowledge, these studies provide the most detailed treatment of methodology employed to measure poverty in the country during transition.

Both studies used survey data collected by the Romanian National Statistical Institute (RNSI) in household surveys. Teşliuc et al. (2003) present consumption-based poverty estimates throughout 1995–2002 using data collected in the RIHS for 1995–2000 and the Romanian Household Budget Survey (RHBS) for 2001–2002. Likewise, Alam et al. (2005) provides consumption-based poverty estimates for 1998–2003 using data from the RIHS for 1998–2000 and from the RHBS for 2001–2003. The strength of the RHBS lies in measuring monthly current consumption, i.e., household purchases of food, non-food, and services as well as self-produced consumption (Teşliuc et al., 2003).

Teşliuc et al. (2003) and Alam et al. (2005) define the following standard poverty estimation parameters to produce poverty estimates. These are presented comparatively below to capture in detail the underlying differences between them.

1. Welfare Indicator

   Both studies use household level consumption. The reason for this option is that the surveys do not report consumption at the individual level. Teşliuc et al. (2003), however, use consumption *per adult equivalent*, while Alam et al. (2005) employ per capita consumption. It is difficult to evaluate precisely the likely biases in the estimation results in and between the two sources that result from these different scales. Nonetheless, per adult, equivalent consumption is generally considered to better capture the consumption level of different individuals within a household (Coudouel, Hentschel, & Wodon, 2001).
2. Welfare Aggregate

   The consumption measure constructed in Teşliuc et al. (2003) includes consumption of food (including self-produced consumption) and purchases of non-food and services and selected durables, but it excludes other services such as publicly provided education, health services, or other in-kind public services. Moreover, it does not include free of charge, in-kind services as the survey does not allow a precise estimation of these items. The consumption aggregate used in Alam et al. (2005), by contrast, is more comprehensive, and it includes some services (such as education) not included in the services category of the aggregate in the other study. It is important to note that poverty has increasingly come to be construed in the literature and practice as a broad, multidimensional concept, seen as both material deprivation (income and/or consumption) and non-material (education, health, leisure, or other services) (Alkire & Foster, 2011; Fusco & Dickes, 2006; Klasen, 2008).
3. Valuing Consumption Items

   In the case of consumption poverty, the aggregate typically includes self-produced consumption that needs to be monetized. In Teşliuc et al. (2003), self-produced consumption is valued on the basis of monthly average prices, while Alam et al. (2005) use median local prices (for the self-produced consumption) and households' own estimation of the value of in-kind transfers and gifts. To account for differences in the cost of living across areas of residence, rural consumption is inflated on the basis of urban prices (due to lower rural prices) using a Laspeyres rural-urban price index constructed from the unit-value information collected in the survey (for the former study). By contrast, Alam et al. (2005) use a Paasche price index to measure spatial price differences arguing that the index involves not only the prices a household pays in relation to the reference prices but also its expenditure pattern, which is not true of a Laspeyres index.
4. Poverty Lines

   Both studies use the cost of basic needs method to set poverty standards separating the poor from the non-poor. Since the analysis in Alam et al. (2005) is not country specific (it incorporates Eastern European and former Soviet Union countries more generally), it uses international poverty lines that are roughly consistent with the national poverty lines commonly used by countries in the region. They use two poverty lines, a \$2.15/day line, which reflects absolute

Table 1.1 Poverty estimates (Alam et al., 2005)

Year	$2.15/day poverty line (%)			$4.30/day poverty line (%)		
	Headcount index	Poverty gap index	Squared poverty gap index	Headcount index	Poverty gap index	Squared poverty gap index
1998	14	3	3	63	21	9
1999	19	4	4	69	25	12
2000	20	5	5	72	26	13
2001	16	4	4	64	22	10
2002	16	4	4	62	22	10
2003	12	3	3	58	19	9

Source: Alam et al. (2005)
Notes: As indicated in Alam et al. (2005), the chapter uses 2000 PPP exchange rates, reported by OECD

material deprivation, and a higher poverty line of $4.30/day, meant to reflect economic vulnerability. Teşliuc et al. (2003) use an extreme poverty line, a food poverty line, and a total poverty line expressed in Romanian Leu (ROL) in December 2002 prices. Each threshold includes an equal food component and an allowance for essential non-food items and services (higher for the total poverty line). The food component is determined on the basis of the cost of a food basket consumed by households from the second and third quintile, valued at the prices faced by these groups. The total poverty line is derived from the food poverty line and is different from the extreme line in that it uses a broader definition of non-food items and services.

5. Poverty Estimates
   Tables 1.1 and 1.2 depict the estimates of poverty measures in the two studies.

They indicate that the estimated incidence of poverty varies between the two sources. Both studies use the standard Foster–Greer–Thorbecke class of poverty measures that is the headcount index (or poverty rate), poverty gap index, and squared poverty gap index (Foster, Greer, & Thorbecke, 1984). Alam et al. (2005) estimated that during 1998–2003, poverty rates in Romania varied from 14% in 1998 to 20% in 2000 and 12% in 2003 for the $2.15/day poverty line and from 63% in 1998 to 72% in 2000 and 58% in 2003 for the $4.30/day threshold. Thus, estimates show that poverty increased in the late 1990s but started to decrease constantly afterwards. Teşliuc et al. (2003) surprisingly found lower poverty estimates (poverty rates of circa 5–6%) using a higher poverty line, with an international equivalent of $2.38/day at 2000 PPP compared to a $2.15/day used in the other study. The estimates in the two studies, however, portray a *broadly* similar picture of the incidence of poverty starting with the early 2000s documenting a decreasing trend. For both time frames, nonetheless, there is variation in the size of estimates.

Table 1.2 Poverty estimates (Teşliuc et al., 2003)

	Food poverty line $2.38/day (%)			Extreme poverty line $2.90/day (%)			Total poverty line $4.20/day (%)		
	Headcount index	Poverty gap index	Squared poverty gap index	Headcount index	Poverty gap index	Squared poverty gap index	Headcount index	Poverty gap index	Squared poverty gap index
1995	5.07	1.03	0.34	9.38	2.10	0.73	25.44	6.73	2.62
1996	2.83	0.50	0.15	6.27	1.20	0.37	20.07	4.77	1.69
1997	5.76	1.16	0.38	11.23	2.46	0.83	30.26	7.93	3.07
1998	5.59	1.13	0.38	11.32	2.41	0.82	30.80	7.97	3.06
1999	6.74	1.37	0.45	12.50	2.83	0.98	33.20	8.80	3.46
2000	7.30	1.42	0.45	13.79	3.02	1.01	35.86	9.57	3.73
2001	5.81	1.15	0.36	11.36	2.47	0.82	30.57	7.92	3.06
2002	5.58	1.14	0.37	10.91	2.39	0.81	28.90	7.59	2.95

Source: Adapted from Teşliuc et al. (2003)

Notes: (1) The food poverty line of 872,005 ROL/adult/month at 2002 prices has an international equivalent of $2.38/adult/day at 2000 PPP rates, (2) The extreme poverty line of 1060, 658 ROL/adult/month at 2002 prices has an international equivalent of $2.90/adult/day at 2000 PPP, (3) The total poverty line of 1,535,570 ROL/adult/month at 2002 prices has an international equivalent of $4.20/adult/day based on 2000 PPP. (Source: Own calculations using the OECD 2000 conversion factors and the CPIs published by the Romanian National Statistical Institute)

1.4 Estimating Poverty from Grouped Distributional Data

Although increasingly available and employed in poverty measurement, there are two main limitations with household survey data: the lack of availability and difficulties in analyzing the large volume of data when data are available (Chen, Datt, & Ravallion, 2007; Minoiu & Reddy, 2008a). These authors argue for the use of grouped data that is data concerning the mean income or expenditure of population shares such as quintiles or deciles as a feasible and reliable alternative to using survey data. Grouped data and an appropriate estimation method are often used in the poverty measurement literature (e.g., Bresson, 2009; Chen & Ravallion, 2001, 2006; Chen & Wang, 2001; Figini & Santarelli, 2006; Karshenas, 2004; Minoiu & Reddy, 2008b; Pritchett, 2006; Son & Kakwani, 2006). The Romanian grouped distributional data used in this chapter reflect monthly total per capita income (or consumption) of deciles of population for 1997–2005.[3] Aggregate consumption and income data are published each year in the Romanian statistical yearbook. The data are provided in Table 1.3 and are expressed in constant 2004 prices (shown in Table 1.4).

Several methods can be employed to estimate the Lorenz curve and obtain poverty measures from grouped data (see, e.g., Minoiu & Reddy, 2008a). One method consists of the parametric estimation of the Lorenz curve. Another approach relies on nonparametric estimation of the income density. The parametric estimation of the Lorenz curve can be reliably used with the software POVCAL, developed and provided by the World Bank. POVCAL is used to produce national poverty estimates in the construction of global poverty assessments when household surveys are not available. The software estimates a Lorenz curve from grouped data using two alternative Lorenz curve specifications that is the generalized quadratic Lorenz curve (the "GQ") proposed by Villasenor and Arnold (1989) and the beta Lorenz curve proposed by Kakwani (1980). As noted by Chen et al. (2007), these two particular parameterizations were implemented in POVCAL as the best options found in the literature. POVCAL estimates the parameters for the two functional forms by transforming them into a linear form and using ordinary least squares regression.

A standard POVCAL output includes the three standard Foster–Greer–Thorbecke poverty measures that is the headcount index of poverty (H), the poverty gap index (PG), and the squared poverty gap index (SPG) for each of the two Lorenz curve specifications for one or more user-specified poverty lines. The headcount index measures the proportion of the population that is poor in the total population. The poverty gap index captures the extent to which individuals or households fall below the poverty line and is expressed as a proportion of the poverty line. It is thus designed to reflect the "depth" of poverty. The squared poverty gap index reflects the "severity" of poverty and is an average of the square of the poverty gaps relative to the poverty line (Foster et al., 1984). The program also provides the elasticity of

[3] The choice between income or consumption is irrelevant in this case because the grouped distributional data in the Romanian statistical yearbooks are identical for each of the ten deciles and are designed to reflect at the same time both income and consumption.

Table 1.3 Total per capita income (consumption), per month

Year	Decile 1	Decile 2	Decile 3	Decile 4	Decile 5	Decile 6	Decile 7	Decile 8	Decile 9	Decile 10
1997	0	123,496	159,776	188,650	217,015	243,833	275,259	314,326	368,720	Over
	123,495	159,769	188,645	217,011	243,829	275,234	314,323	368,719	469,424	469,464
1998	0	258,798	333,887	393,782	450,583	507,907	573,966	656,042	769,742	Over
	258,796	333,824	393,777	450,571	507,901	573,961	656,009	769,581	986,694	986,728
1999	0	322,047	421,004	503,639	581,499	661,034	752,097	860,721	1,011,586	Over
	322,034	420,989	503,637	581,491	661,008	752,093	860,715	1,011,580	1,284,628	1,284,708
2000	0	494,197	644,709	763,803	877,661	995,541	1,131,127	1,302,212	1,547,702	Over
	493,968	644,623	763,779	877,628	995,541	1,131,120	1,302,195	1,547,685	1,978,378	1,978,703
2001	0	340,454	544,144	725,605	896,273	1,085,352	1,295,877	1,550,766	1,905,849	Over
	340,440	544,038	725,581	896,259	1,085,337	1,295,865	1,550,758	1,905,555	2,555,641	2,555,747
2002	0	467,445	734,431	975,518	1,219,560	1,487,723	1,762,947	2,106,423	2,597,936	Over
	467,376	734,428	975,498	1,219,424	1,487,589	1,762,542	2,106,301	2,597,784	3,545,714	3,545,750
2003	0	603,502	922,675	1,204,614	1,505,267	1,840,000	2,169,896	2,569,174	3,154,121	Over
	603,500	922,674	1,204,414	1,504,684	1,839,738	2,169,859	2,569,142	3,153,805	4,313,736	4,314,028
2004	0	873,074	1,288,892	1,654,500	2,023,706	2,439,301	2,886,907	3,436,003	4,242,346	Over
	873,000	1,288,889	1,654,296	2,023,512	2,439,258	2,886,835	3,435,951	4,242,111	5,802,064	5,802,298
2005	0	104	152	195	241	289	340	404	500	Over
	104	152	195	241	289	340	404	500	688	689

Source: Romanian statistical yearbooks, 1998–2006, Romanian National Statistical Institute

Notes: (1) The grouped distributional data in the statistical yearbooks is identical for both income and consumption, (2) Figures are expressed in ROL (Romanian Leu) except for 2005 when they are provided in RON (Romanian New Leu). The equivalent of 1 RON is 10,000 ROL, (3) For each year, the upper row indicates the lower bound of the interval, while the lower row stands for the upper bound, (4) Amounts for each of the 9 years are expressed in January prices of that year (e.g., 2000 amounts are expressed in January 2000 prices)

Table 1.4 Total per capita income (consumption), per month in constant 2004 prices

Year	Decile 1	Decile 2	Decile 3	Decile 4	Decile 5	Decile 6	Decile 7	Decile 8	Decile 9	Decile 10
1997	0	886,547	1,146,992	1,354,271	1,557,897	1,750,416	1,976,016	2,256,468	2,646,949	Over
	886,540	1,146,942	1,354,235	1,557,870	1,750,388	1,975,836	2,256,447	2,646,942	3,369,878	3,370,165
1998	0	1,167,861	1,506,710	1,776,995	2,033,317	2,291,999	2,590,099	2,960,478	3,473,565	Over
	1,167,852	1,506,426	1,776,972	2,033,263	2,291,972	2,590,077	2,960,329	3,472,838	4,452,590	4,452,744
1999	0	996,741	1,303,015	1,558,771	1,799,749	2,045,911	2,327,753	2,663,946	3,130,876	Over
	996,701	1,302,968	1,558,765	1,799,725	2,045,831	2,327,741	2,663,928	3,130,857	3,975,946	3,976,193
2000	0	1,050,142	1,369,972	1,623,041	1,864,983	2,115,472	2,403,584	2,767,131	3,288,785	Over
	1,049,656	1,369,790	1,622,990	1,864,913	2,115,472	2,403,570	2,767,095	3,288,748	4,203,948	4,204,639
2001	0	538,012	859,899	1,146,658	1,416,361	1,715,158	2,047,846	2,450,642	3,011,771	Over
	537,990	859,731	1,146,620	1,416,338	1,715,134	2,047,827	2,450,629	3,011,307	4,038,624	4,038,791
2002	0	602,844	947,164	1,258,084	1,572,814	1,918,652	2,273,597	2,716,563	3,350,446	Over
	602,755	947,160	1,258,058	1,572,639	1,918,479	2,273,075	2,716,406	3,350,250	4,572,755	4,572,801
2003	0	675,209	1,032,306	1,347,744	1,684,121	2,058,626	2,427,720	2,874,439	3,528,889	Over
	675,207	1,032,305	1,347,521	1,683,468	2,058,333	2,427,678	2,874,404	3,528,535	4,826,288	4,826,614
2004	0	873,074	1,288,892	1,654,500	2,023,706	2,439,301	2,886,907	3,436,003	4,242,346	Over
	873,000	1,288,889	1,654,296	2,023,512	2,439,258	2,886,835	3,435,951	4,242,111	5,802,064	5,802,298
2005	0	95.42	139.46	178.92	221.12	265.16	311.96	370.68	458.76	Over
	95.42	139.46	178.92	221.12	265.16	311.96	370.68	458.76	631.25	632.17

Source: Author's calculations using the grouped data provided in the Romanian statistical yearbooks and RNSI's CPIs

Notes: (1) The grouped data in the statistical yearbooks is identical for both income and consumption, (2) Figures are expressed in ROL (Romanian Leu) except for 2005 when they are provided in RON (Romanian New Leu). The equivalent of 1 RON is 10,000 ROL. All data is expressed in constant 2004 prices, (3) For each year, the upper row indicates the lower bound of the interval, while the lower row stands for the upper bound the three poverty measures with respect to the mean income. Based on goodness-of-fit criteria, POVCAL determines which of the two specifications better fits the data. POVCAL requires that the grouped distributional data be set up in one of the eight ways in which the software can read the data.[4] The Romanian data is of data type eight that is the upper bound of a class interval (UBCI) and percentage of the population in a given income interval f(x). As noted in the POVCAL tutorial, data type eight does not provide information on the mean income of each interval, which implies that the software needs to estimate the means in order to produce the Lorenz curve and the poverty estimates. The lack of the means of intervals will result in some loss of accuracy, but the rule gave trustworthy results in experiments according to the tutorial accompanying the program. The dataset as used in POVCAL is provided in Table 1.5.

1.5 Results

Table 1.6 presents the poverty estimates on the basis of six poverty lines, chosen to allow for comparison with the poverty lines used in the two studies reviewed earlier. The $2.15/day and $4.30/day poverty lines are the two poverty lines used in Alam et al. (2005), while the $2.38/day, $2.90/day, and $4.20/day poverty lines are the international equivalents of the three poverty lines used in Teşliuc et al. (2003).[5]

Overall, the estimates reflect two different narratives of the extent and dynamics of poverty in Romania during transition. On the one hand, during 1997–2000, the poverty rate was highly irregular, while, on the other hand, during 2001–2005 it decreased constantly throughout the period. Therefore, in what follows, the estimates will be discussed separately for the two time periods.

(a) The dark age of transition. High irregularity of poverty estimates (1997–2001)

    Poverty shrank significantly in 1998 compared to the previous year, increased in 1999 compared to 1998 (but was still below the 1997 levels), and decreased by 2–3 percentage points in 2000 compared to 1999. The depth of poverty (measured by the poverty gap index) fluctuated, depending on changes in the poverty rate from 3.23% in 1997 to 1.68% in 2000 (for the $2.15/day threshold) indicating that overall the poor approached the poverty line significantly during the period. The squared poverty gap index also decreased to 0.55% in 2000 compared to 1.15% in 1997 (for the $2.15 poverty line) and from 9.45% to 6.02% (for the $4.30 threshold), reflecting a high level of severe poverty for the latter poverty line (Table 1.6).

(b) The second stage of transition. Declining poverty trend (2002–2005)

---

[4] More information about POVCAL, including a detailed tutorial, is available at (http://iresearch.worldbank.org/PovcalNet/index.htm).

[5] In addition to these five poverty lines, we used the extreme $1.08/day poverty line, typical in international measurements of poverty in developing countries.

Table 1.5 Grouped distributional data as used in POVCAL, constant 2004 prices

1997	1998	1999	2000	2001	2002	2003	2004	2005	
UBCI	UBCI	UBCI	UBCI	UBCI	UBCI	UBCI	UBCI	UBCI	f(x)
886,540	1,167,852	996,701	1,049,656	537,990	602,755	675,207	873,000	95.42	0.1
1,146,942	1,506,426	1,302,968	1,369,790	859,731	947,160	1,032,305	1,288,889	139.46	0.1
1,354,235	1,776,972	1,558,765	1,622,990	1,146,620	1,258,058	1,347,521	1,654,296	178.92	0.1
1,557,870	2,033,263	1,799,725	1,864,913	1,416,338	1,572,639	1,683,468	2,023,512	221.12	0.1
1,750,388	2,291,972	2,045,831	2,115,472	1,715,134	1,918,479	2,058,333	2,439,258	265.16	0.1
1,975,836	2,590,077	2,327,741	2,403,570	2,047,827	2,273,075	2,427,678	2,886,835	311.96	0.1
2,256,447	2,960,329	2,663,928	2,767,095	2,450,629	2,716,406	2,874,404	3,435,951	370.68	0.1
2,646,942	3,472,838	3,130,857	3,288,748	3,011,307	3,350,250	3,528,535	4,242,111	458.76	0.1
3,369,878	4,452,590	3,975,946	4,203,948	4,038,624	4,572,755	4,826,288	5,802,064	631.25	0.1
8,369,878	9,452,590	8,975,946	9,203,948	9,038,624	9,572,755	9,826,288	10,802,064	1131.25	0.1

Source: Author's calculations using grouped data from the Romanian statistical yearbooks, 1998–2006 and RNSI's CPIs

Figures are expressed in ROL (Romanian Leu) except for 2005 when they are provided in RON (Romanian New Leu). The equivalent of 1 RON is 10,000 ROL. UBCI stands for the upper bound of each income interval; f(x) is the proportion of the population in each category that is 10% throughout

Table 1.6 Poverty estimates from grouped data, 1997–2005

	$1.08/day poverty line			$2.15/day poverty line			$4.30/day poverty line			$2.38/day food poverty line			$2.90/day extreme poverty line			$4.20/day total poverty line		
Year	H	PG	SPG	H	PG	SPG	H	PG	SPG	H	PG	SPG	H	PG	SPG	H	PG	SPG
1997	Nwab	Nwab	Nwab	14.66	3.23	1.15	61.40	20.79	9.45	19.60	4.57	1.65	30.96	8.28	3.09	59.52	19.84	8.93
1998	Nwab	Nwab	Nwab	5.58	1.12	0.41	39.80	11.39	4.53	8.28	1.67	0.59	15.96	3.52	1.23	38.04	10.73	4.21
1999	Nwab	Nwab	Nwab	10.01	2.11	0.74	48.94	15.61	6.83	13.75	3.05	1.08	23.16	5.80	2.16	47.13	14.84	6.42
2000	Nwab	Nwab	Nwab	8.52	1.68	0.55	46.17	14.25	6.02	12.04	2.51	0.84	21.05	5.01	1.78	44.39	13.51	5.64
2001	7.53	1.67	0.52	25.53	9.20	4.49	59.29	26.20	15.11	29.48	10.97	5.52	38.30	15.08	7.99	57.98	25.43	14.59
2002	5.63	1.04	0.27	22.81	7.61	3.40	53.48	22.92	12.94	26.38	9.25	4.33	33.55	12.83	6.62	52.19	22.21	12.47
2003	3.79	0.58	0.13	19.98	6.17	2.57	49.89	20.58	11.26	23.44	7.67	3.37	31.05	11.18	5.36	48.59	19.89	10.83
2004	0.48	0.01	0.00	12.97	3.29	1.12	40.07	14.92	7.43	15.83	4.36	1.62	22.42	7.01	2.95	38.85	14.34	7.08
2005	Nwab	Nwab	Nwab	12.98	3.30	1.13	35.87	12.91	6.24	13.42	3.47	1.21	19.42	5.79	2.33	34.71	12.38	5.93

Source: Author's calculations using POVCAL

(1) All poverty measures are expressed in percentage form: H stands for the headcount index of poverty (poverty rate), PG for the poverty gap index, and SPG for the squared poverty gap index, (2) The $2.15/day and $4.30/day poverty lines are the two poverty lines used in Alam et al. (2005). The $2.38/day, $2.90/day, and $4.20/day poverty lines are the international equivalents of the three poverty lines used in Teşliuc et al. (2003), (3) "nwab" stands for "not within admissible bounds" and it means that the poverty line inputted in POVCAL is outside the required range estimated by the program

The estimates indicate that throughout 2002–2005, poverty decreased considerably, which is in line with the other estimates found in the literature. The declining trend is in contrast with the irregular estimates found for the 1997–2000 period. Nearly 13% of the population was living below the \$2.15/day threshold in 2005, compared to close to 20% in 2003 and 26% in 2001. The poverty gap index shrank from 9.20% in 2001 to 3.30% in 2005 and from 26.20% in 2001 to 12.91% in 2005 (for the \$4.30/day threshold) reflecting a high gap between the welfare level of the poor and the poverty line (Table 1.6).

On the whole, examining the poverty estimates over the entire period, 2001 may be considered a nodal point. In 2001, the poverty measures rose abruptly reflecting a *much* higher poverty compared to the previous year. Starting with 2002, poverty decreased constantly.

1.6 Conclusions and Discussion

This chapter first compared transitional Romanian poverty estimates and their underlying methodologies as found in the literature. Then it provided a new set of estimates of poverty during the early and late transition, including a two-year period not covered by the literature. The chapter used grouped distributional data, reflecting the upper bounds of intervals and the proportion of population in each category.

The estimates derived from grouped distributional data indicate that poverty was highly irregular throughout 1997–2000. This finding partially supports the results in the literature. During 2002–2005 the incidence of poverty dropped considerably, which is broadly consistent with the declining trend estimated elsewhere in the literature. We found that 2001 was a crucial year, which coincided with the start of a decreasing poverty trend.

What can explain the sudden and significant changes in poverty estimated for 2001? There are two possible explanations. First, they may reflect actual changes in the incidence of poverty, and second, they may reflect changes pertaining to the survey design, or to the methodology employed in aggregating the individual data. In 2001, the Household Budget Survey replaced the Integrated Household Survey, which may have introduced a variation in the design and data collection methods. However, they are considered to be comparable (Teşliuc et al., 2003). Although it is likely that the estimates were affected to some extent by the use of different methodologies, this is unlikely to have resulted in large biases. The evidence that starting with 2001, poverty measures are constantly decreasing, while throughout 1997–2000 they were highly irregular, may indicate an improvement in the survey design or in the aggregation methodology. Nonetheless, it is unlikely that biases are significant. It is more likely that the two different stories of the early and late transition are associated with the positive changes in the economic condition of the country than with methodological or data deficiencies.

The comparison of estimates both from the literature and those estimated in this chapter indicate significant differences in the actual extent of poverty, giving rise to further questions about the limits of poverty measurement and estimation in a transition context. It is not surprising that *some* differences in the size of estimates exist, considering that different methods and data are used. However, these differences are by no means small in size. Consider, for example, estimates for 1998 for a relatively comparable poverty line ($2.15/day). The estimated poverty rate introduced in this chapter is virtually identical to the one estimated in part of the literature (5.5% in 1998) but differs sharply from 14% estimated elsewhere in the literature. Clearly, these are not small differences. It is not the same to say that 5% or 14%, respectively, of a population of a country lives below $2.15/day. The same observation can be made for other years. The key finding here is that there are significant differences between presumably comparable poverty estimates—regardless of whether these are derived on the basis of unit record data or grouped data. The results we reach from this comparison are not easy to explain. The broadly similar trend aside, the estimates from the literature based on survey data do not point to the same size of poverty in transitional Romania. Likewise, we did not find that estimates from grouped data indicate a radically different story—there are greater differences between estimates based on survey data than between those introduced here from grouped data and existing ones derived from survey data. Additional research is needed to understand the effect that certain parameters and definitions employed to estimate poverty have on the ensuing estimates.

These findings have broader implications for poverty research. These implications pertain to the use of grouped data and Lorenz curve interpolation in poverty measurement. Based on the Romanian case documented here, we find support for the use of this method. We found that there is a need to use this approach even when survey data are available, since estimates derived from survey data may indicate different stories of the extent of poverty. In such cases, the method may be used efficiently to provide further documentation on the size of poverty. In cases when survey data are not available—which is frequently the case—grouped data-based estimation is the only available approach. While limited compared to the wealth of information that can be obtained from survey data, in terms of estimation of poverty measures, we find no qualitative difference between this method and those based on survey data.

Acknowledgments I would like to acknowledge the invaluable support of Monica Silaghi and Camelia Minoiu during the writing of the thesis on which this contribution is based. Recently, Camelia Minoiu, Christopher Pollitt, and Greg Porumbescu reviewed an earlier draft and provided a number of helpful comments.

References

Alam, A., Murthi, M., Yemtsov, R., Murrugarra, E., Dudwick, N., Hamilton, E., et al. (2005). *Growth, poverty and inequality: Eastern Europe and the former soviet union*. Washington, DC: Europe and Central Asia Region World Bank.

Alkire, S., & Foster, J. (2011). Counting and multidimensional poverty measurement. *Journal of Public Economics, 95*, 476–487.

Bresson, F. (2009). On the estimation of growth and inequality elasticities of poverty with grouped data. *Review of Income and Wealth, 55*(2), 266–302.

Chen, S., Datt, G., & Ravallion, M. (2007). *POVCAL, a program for calculating poverty measures from grouped data*. DEC-RG, World Bank: Washington, DC.

Chen, S., & Ravallion, M. (2001). How did the world's poorest fare in the 1990s? *Review of Income and Wealth, 47*(3), 283–300.

Chen, S., & Ravallion, M. (2006). China's (uneven) progress against poverty. *Journal of Development Economics, 82*(1), 1–42.

Chen, S., & Wang, Y. (2001). *China's growth and poverty reduction: recent trends between 1990 and 1999* (World Bank Policy Research Working Paper No. 2651), Washington, DC: World Bank.

Coudouel, A., Hentschel, J. S., & Wodon, Q. T. (2001). Poverty measurement and analysis with Annex A: Technical notes. In J. Klugman (Ed.), *Poverty reduction strategy sourcebook*. Washington, DC: World Bank.

Figini, P., & Santarelli, E. (2006). Openness, economic reforms, and poverty: Globalization in the developing countries. *Journal of Developing Areas, 39*(2), 129–151.

Foster, J., Greer, J., & Thorbecke, E. (1984). A class of decomposable poverty measures. *Econometrica, 52*(3), 761–766.

Fusco, A., & Dickes, P. (2006). *Rasch model and multidimensional poverty measurement* (IRISS Working Paper 2006-02). Differdange, Luxembourg: CEPS/INSTEAD.

Kakwani, N. (1980). On a class of poverty measures. *Econometrica, 48*(2), 437–446.

Karshenas, M. (2004). *Global poverty estimates and the millennium goals: Towards a unified framework* (ILO Employment Strategy Paper No. 2004/5). Geneva, Switzerland: International Labor Organization.

Klasen, S. (2008). Economic growth and poverty reduction: Measurement issues using income and non-income indicators. *World Development, 36*(3), 420–445.

Milanovic, B. (1998). *Income, inequality and poverty during the transition from planned to market economy*. World Bank: Washington, DC.

Minoiu, C., & Reddy, S. G. (2008a). Estimating poverty and inequality from grouped data: How well do parametric methods perform? *Journal of Income Distribution, 18*(2), 24.

Minoiu, C., & Reddy, S. G. (2008b). Chinese poverty: Assessing the impact of alternative assumptions. *Review of Income and Wealth, 54*(4), 572–596.

Molnar, M. (2000). Poverty measurement and income support in Romania. In S. Hutton & G. Redmond (Eds.), *Poverty in transition economies*. London: Routledge.

Pritchett, L. (2006). Who is not poor? Dreaming of a world truly free of poverty. *The World Bank Research Observer, 21*(1), 1–23.

Son, H. H., & Kakwani, N. (2006). *Global estimates of pro-poor growth* (UNDP–IPC Working Paper No. 31). Brasilia, Brazil: United Nations Development Programme: International Poverty Center.

Subbarao, K., & Mehra, K. (1995). *Social assistance and the poor in Romania* (Education and social policy discussion paper series No. 66). Washington, DC: World Bank.

Teşliuc, E., Pop, L., & Panduru, F. (2003). *Poverty in Romania: Profile and trends during 1995–2002* (In: World Bank, Romania Poverty Assessment Volume II: Background Papers, Report No. 26169-RO). Washington, DC: Europe and Central Asia Region, World Bank.

Villasenor, J. A., & Arnold, B. C. (1989). Elliptical Lorenz curves. *Journal of Econometrics, 40*, 327–338.

World Bank. (1997). *Romania: Poverty and social policy* (Report No. 16462-RO, in two volumes: Volume 1 Main Report and Volume 2 Statistical Annex). Washington, DC: World Bank.

Chapter 2
An Empirical Analysis of Herzberg's Two-Factor od Work Motivation Applied on Hospital Employees in Jordan

Adriana AnaMaria Davidescu

Abstract The objective of this study is to identify the main motivational factors for employees from Jordanian private and public hospitals to see what kind of factors will manifest a higher impact on the overall level of motivation. Also, the paper aims to analyze the potential differences in the opinions of employees from the public vs. private hospitals regarding the main growth and hygiene motivational factors. A structural equation model was used to empirically test the Herzberg's two-factor theory of work motivation. This study is based on a sample of 325 employees from 6 hospitals in Jordan.

The findings of research support the two-factor theory of work motivation, revealing that both hygiene and growth motivation factors manifest a positive impact on the overall degree of motivation.

The empirical results revealed that growth factors manifested a higher impact on the overall level of motivation comparative with the hygiene factors, but both of them generate increasing the level of motivation.

Regarding the hygiene factors, rewards have a higher impact on motivation, while the well-defined mission statement of the company, having the necessary information for performing tasks, and receiving vocational education at the workplace are considered to be the growth factors with a highest impact on overall motivation of employees.

Analyzing the differences between employees from private and public hospitals regarding the main motivational factors, it is worth to mention that there are not statistical differences between the opinions of employees from public and private

A.A. Davidescu, Ph.D. (✉)
Department of Statistics and Econometrics, Bucharest Academy of Economic Studies, Bucharest, Romania

Department of Labour Market Policies, National Research Institute for Labour and Social Protection, Bucharest, Romania
e-mail: adrianaalexandru@yahoo.com

S. Văduva et al. (eds.), *Solutions for Business, Culture and Religion in Eastern Europe and Beyond*, DOI 10.1007/978-3-319-63369-5_2

hospitals regarding wage, rewards or interpersonal relations, highlighting that not financial incentives are the main reason for the decision of people to work in a private hospital.

But regarding the growth factors, employees from private hospitals in Jordan declared to be more motivated by having a listener of their ideas, thoughts and suggestions, by receiving encouragement or receiving training for their tasks.

This implies that in order to get motivated employees, management needs to give their employees knowledge, information and training. By creating such a context, the intrinsic value of employees is likely to improve, and they will be able to advance in their occupational role.

Keywords Hygiene factors • Growth factors • Hospitals • Health workers • Survey • Jordan • Structural equation models

2.1 Introduction

Hospital performance is deeply influenced by the quality of human resources. It can be directly influenced by the improvement of employees' skills and indirectly by increasing employee motivation.

The lack of motivation of health personnel constitutes a main preoccupation of the health system in Jordan, and there are a lot of national studies which investigated the influential factors of the retention mainly for nurses.

The paper aims to identify the main motivational factors for the employees from Jordanian private and public hospitals to see what kind of factors will manifest a higher impact on the overall level of motivation using an adapted version of the growth-hygiene factor theory of Herzberg proposed by Lundberg, Gudmundson, and Andersson (2009). In order to do that, there will be used structural equation models, Mann-Whitney test and descriptive statistics.

The study will take into consideration the opinions of 325 employees from 6 public and private Jordanian hospitals, the data being collected in 2015.

The main advantage of this study comparative with the others is the fact that it reflects the opinions of several categories of employees, doctors, nurses, administrative staff, support staff, helpers and others highlighting existing differences related to the main sources of motivation.

2.2 Literature Review

Among Jordanian hospitals, the nursing deficit is indeed an important issue, investigated in several national studies (Franco, Bennett, Kanfer, & Stubblebine, 2004, Mrayyan, 2005, 2008, Mrayyan & Al-Faouri, 2008, Saleh, Darawad, & Al-Hussami, 2014, AbuAlRub, Omari, & Al-Zaru, 2009, AbuAlRub & Al-Zaru, 2008).

Lambrou, Kontodimopoulos, and Niakas (2010) proved that achievement was voted to be the main driver of motivation by the employees from Nicosia General Hospital in Cyprus, revealing that there are differences regarding financial incentives in public vs. private hospitals and that nurses tended to be more motivated than the medical staff. Also the analysis of potential differences regarding motivation sources among health professionals in Greece confirmed that achievement was regarded to be very important for the employees of this sector and the degree of motivation is significantly higher in private hospitals comparative with public hospitals in Greece (Kontodimopoulos, Paleologou, & Niakas, 2009).

The study of Franco et al. (2004) pointed out the importance of nonfinancial incentives in the increase of the level of overall motivation, even in the case of two different countries Georgia and Jordan. Mrayyan (2005) analyzed the level of satisfaction among nurses from public and private Jordanian hospitals, pointing out a higher level of satisfaction among nurses from private hospitals and also a higher intention of retention. AbuAlRub et al. (2009) also confirmed the previous result in the case of Jordanian hospitals, mentioning also that social support has an important impact on the level of satisfaction and intention to stay among nurses. The determinants of the intention to stay have been investigated by the AbuAlRub (2010), who mentioned that support from co-workers and supervisors tends to increase the intention of nurses to stay at the current workplace.

Mrayyan (2008) mentioned the organizational climate from the hospital, organizational structure and also the age as the factors that most likely could influence the intention to stay of Jordanian nurses.

Saleh et al. (2014) pointed out relevant results using the perceptions of nurses from eight Jordanian hospitals revealing that ward nurses exhibit a higher level of work satisfaction and organizational commitment comparative with unit nurses.

Al-Faouri, Al-Ali, and Al-Shorman (2014) take into consideration the potential role of emotional intelligence on the level of satisfaction of Jordanian nurses, revealing that it could be seen as a potential driver in the process of increasing the level of satisfaction.

Highlighting the potential differences across government, teaching and private hospitals in Jordan regarding the nurses' performance at work, Mrayyan and Al-Faouri (2008) demonstrated a higher level of performance in private hospitals and also a possible relationship with career commitment.

Despite the fact that financial incentives play an important role in the process of motivation of employees in general, nonfinancial instruments have their place well established in increasing the level of motivation and also the intention to stay.

2.3 Methodology and Data

The main objective of the paper is to highlight the main motivational factors of Jordanian hospital employees taking into consideration the characteristics of Herzberg's two-factor theory, having as starting point the paper of Lundberg et al. (2009). The importance of the study resides in identifying the factors that could generate a win-win situation for both employee and organization and if the intrinsic factors could be more important for the satisfaction of employees than the hygiene factors.

In order to improve the performance of healthcare system, it is important to know the nonfinancial factors that could increase the satisfaction and also the performance of employees.

According to Herzberg (1971) and Herzberg, Mausner, and Bloch Snyderman (2005), individuals have "two different sets of needs and that the different elements of the work situation satisfies or dissatisfies these needs. While the first set includes factors related most likely to working conditions- policy-reward system, salary, job security and interpersonal relations- hygiene (dissatisfaction) factors, the second set of factors includes factors related to the work itself, -recognition, achievement, responsibility, advancement and work itself- satisfaction factors".

It is worth to mention that the presence of satisfaction factors called also "intrinsic motivators" most likely increases the level of motivation, while the presence of dissatisfaction factors called also "extrinsic motivators" most likely prevents dissatisfaction, but they are responsible for the increase of the satisfaction level.

This kind of theory has been applied in analyzing the main determinants of work motivation at the level of different countries and different areas like education, electricity industry, online sales, pharmaceutical sales, criminology, construction industry, tourism industry, etc.

Band, Shah, Sriram, and Appliances (2016) applied two-factor theory to identify the main intrinsic and extrinsic factors in educational field, revealing that achievement is the most important intrinsic motivational factor among management faculty employees, while job security and working conditions were mentioned as the most important among the extrinsic factors.

Muslim, Dean, and Cohen (2016) proved by applying the Herzberg's theory on the employees of an electricity provider company in Malaysia that the environment is one of the most important motivational factors for the job search.

This theory of motivation was surprisingly applied in identifying the factors that could activate the online impulse buying. According to the results obtained by Lo, Lin, and Hsu (2016), sales promotion is considered to be the motivational factor that could increase the online impulse buying, while the design factors of online stores were identified to be the extrinsic factors.

The theory has found its applicability also in the field of pharmaceutical sales; the study of Sanjeev and Surya (2016) confirms the statement of Herzberg according to which the intrinsic factors are responsible to the increase of satisfaction level, while the extrinsic factors do not manifest any impact on the satisfaction level.

There is empirical evidence in the literature of the application of this theory even on measuring the satisfaction level of law enforcement officers. Singer (2016) proved using the Kruskal-Wallis test and the principal component analysis that there are not statistical significant differences for different levels of education of the officers or for supervisory vs. non-supervisory officers concerning both hygiene and satisfaction factors or the overall level of satisfaction.

Ruthankoon and Olu Ogunlana (2003) demonstrated that the theory does not prove its whole applicability on the Thai construction industry, mentioning that achievement is a motivational driver for engineers, but it generates both satisfaction and dissatisfaction for foremen.

Finally, it is important to mention also the paper of Lundberg et al. (2009), who analyze the main sources of motivation for seasonal employees from the tourism area divided into two subgroups—migrants and residents—using structural equation models under the Herzberg's theory. The main results pointed out that the need for meeting new people is more important for migrants, while the level of salary could be seen as a generator of a higher level of satisfaction for residents.

Therefore, even if this theory of motivation draws several criticisms over the last decades, the two-factor theory has found its applicability in the last decades in different fields, topics and contexts.

In the present paper, an adapted version of Herzberg's theory provided by Lundberg et al. (2009) will be applied, who take into account three hygiene factors (wage, rewards and interpersonal relations), four growth factors (responsibility, recognition, knowledge and information) and also motivation sources, summing a total of 19 items measured on a 5-point Likert-type scale format, where "1 is very dissatisfied" and "5 is very satisfied".

The hygiene factors are quantified using one item each, while the four growth factors are determined as follows: responsibility (two items), recognition (three items), knowledge (four items), information (three items) and motivation (four items).

In the analysis, a sample of 325 employees from 6 Jordanian hospitals was used: King Abdullah, Al-Shona and Princess Basma public hospitals and Amman, Irbid and Ibn Al-Nafees private hospitals. The data was collected in period July–September 2015.

As methods used in identifying the main motivational factors of Jordanian hospital employees, the structural equation models considering three latent variables such as work motivation, hygiene factors and growth factors will be used, taking into account multiple factors and multiple effects of the "these latent variables".

According to Schneider et al. (2010, p. 9–10), "this model presents the statistical relationships between the latent variables and the observed variables, using the covariance matrix of them". The model has two kinds of equations, the structural model—which revealed the relationships among the latent variables and motivational determinants—and measurement model—which links motivational proxies with the latent variables.

In structural equations modelling (SEM), all statistical tests and indicators are used to determine how well the model fits to the data, by analyzing the discrepancy between expected and observed covariance matrices. The maximum likelihood method is used for the estimation of the parameters.

In order to identify the optimal model, the following criteria were used in the analysis: the statistical significance of the parameters using t-test, the validity of the model using chi-square test, the value of root mean square error of approximation

(RMSEA), the value of standardized root mean square residual (SRMR), the value of coefficient of determination (CD) and the value of tucker lewis index (TLI) and comparative fit index (CFI).

In order to test the differences between private and public hospitals concerning the main growth and hygiene factors, Mann-Whitney test was applied.

Stata software version 13 was used to build, estimate and test the structural equation model and the validity of the theory and also to test the existence of statistical differences among motivational factors.

2.4 Empirical Results

2.4.1 Sample Profile

Analyzing the sample profile of respondents, we can reveal the following:

- The majority of respondents come from public hospitals (66.5%).
- Most of them are men (52.9%).
- About half of them belong to the age group (25–35 years) (51.4%).
- The majority has a bachelor degree in science (43.3%).
- About 70.2% of the respondents are married.
- About 40% of them have a work experience of 10 years in the hospital, and most of them (51.5%) work in the therapeutic area.
- Regarding the distribution of employees by category, the majority (36%) are nurses, while the proportion of doctors is only 19% from all respondents.
- About 71% of the respondents do not have any management position;
- As the main changes that could affect hospitals, heavy workload was pointed out by the majority of the respondents (43.6%).
- About 62.5% of respondents declared to have more than 20 patients per day.

2.4.2 Main Results of the Measurement Model of Work Motivation

Analyzing the responses of hospital employees regarding hygiene and growth motivational factors and also the main proxies for motivation, presented in Table 2.1, the results revealed that:

- Among the hygiene factors, the factor considered by the employees as having the highest potential in preventing dissatisfaction was interpersonal relationships and the necessity to meet new people, while at opposite side, rewards were considered to generate the highest level of dissatisfaction.

Table 2.1 Descriptive statistics of the variables

Variable	Mean	Std. dev.
Hygiene factors		
Wage	2.86	1.19
Rewards	2.76	1.15
Interpersonal relationships	**3.17**	1.07
Growth factors		
Resp.1	**3.55**	1.03
Resp.2	**3.61**	1.03
Recog.1	3.31	1.07
Recog.2	3.00	1.11
Recog.3	2.94	1.11
Know.1	3.06	1.13
Know.2	**3.62**	1.07
Know.3	**3.57**	1.00
Know.4	3.22	1.12
Info.1	3.35	1.11
Info.2	3.40	1.07
Info.3	3.12	1.07
Motivation sources		
Motiv.1	2.80	1.18
Motiv.2	3.00	1.24
Motiv.3	**3.21**	1.11
Motiv.4	3.09	1.18

Bold figures revealed the factors with the highest score, pointing out the main determinants among hygiene and growth factors

- Among growth factors, the responses of respondents highlighted as main motivational factors, having necessary skills, having the knowledge to take decisions and having a certain level of responsibility in the job.
- Among different sources for the overall level of motivation, the most respondents considered to be most likely motivated by the co-workers and they are least motivated by management.

In order to measure the latent variable work motivation for the total sample, answers to four questions were used as manifest variables, having the assumption that if the latent variable influences manifest variables; thus, if a worker is motivated, answers to these questions will be positive. The standardized estimates of the coefficients are presented in Fig. 2.1 revealing that all manifest variables are significantly related to the latent construct work motivation.

Analyzing the standardized coefficients of all manifest variables, it is worth to mention that highest level of motivation is received from managers (motiv.2; 0.81), followed by the level of motivation received from management (motiv.1; 0.69). The chi-square test of the overall model fit registered a value of 3.19 with a p-value of more than 0.10, revealing an acceptable level of model fit. The value of RMSEA is

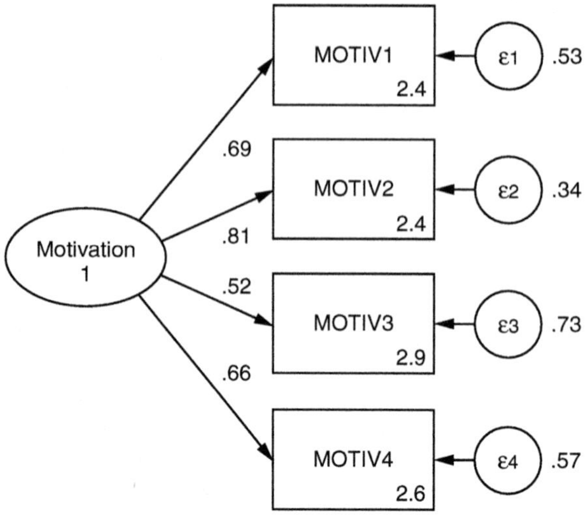

Fig. 2.1. The measurement model uses four manifest variables to measure the latent variable work motivation. Note: Chi2(2) = 3.19, Prob > chi2 = 0.20, RMSEA = 0.043, Pclose (probability that RMSEA<=0.05) = 0.442, comparative fit index (CFI) = 0.996, Tucker-Lewis index (TLI) = 0.989, SRMR = 0.016, CD = 0.799

very small and the probability is very high indicating a good model fit. The coefficient of determination of 0.799 revealed that 79.9% of total variation in the overall motivation could be explained by all the manifest variables. The small value of SRMR indicates a good model. A good model fit is pointed out also by the values of comparative fit index (CFI) and Tucker-Lewis index (TLI), whose values are much closed to one.

2.4.3 The Structural Model of Work Motivation Among Hospital Workers

In order to test empirically the validity of Herzberg's theory on hospital employees, a structural equation model was applied using the individual constructs of all hygiene and growth factors. The empirical results of standardized coefficients are presented in the Table 2.2.

All items for both growth and hygiene factors were determined to be statistically significant at 1% level of significance, supporting the validity of the Herzberg's theory on the health system in Jordan. Figure 2.2 shows the path diagram of the model. Analyzing the standardized coefficients, growth factors manifested a higher impact on the overall level of motivation comparative with the hygiene factors, but both of them generate increasing level of motivation. From the category of hygiene factors, measured by three items, rewards manifest the highest impact on the level of motivation.

In the category of growth factors measured by 12 items, the most important factors that are associated with a higher level of motivation are the well-defined mission statement of the company (Info.1), having the necessary information for

Table 2.2 The empirical results of structural equation model

Variable	Standardized coefficients
Hygiene factors	0.22[a]
Wage	0.78[a]
Rewards	0.89[a]
Interpersonal relationships	0.56[a]
Growth factors	0.67[a]
Resp.1	0.54[a]
Resp.2	0.57[a]
Recog.1	0.55[a]
Recog.2	0.51[a]
Recog.3	0.47[a]
Know.1	0.58[a]
Know.2	0.55[a]
Know.3	0.54[a]
Know.4	0.63[a]
Info.1	0.68[a]
Info.2	0.66[a]
Info.3	0.59[a]
Motiv.1	0.67[a]
Motiv.2	0.73[a]
Motiv.3	0.54[a]
Motiv.4	0.66[a]

[a]Statistical significance at the 1% level of significance

performing tasks (Info.2) and receiving vocational education at the workplace (Know.4). At the opposite side, the level of receiving encouragement when setting goals was the factor with the smallest impact on the increase of the overall level of motivation.

2.4.4 Analyzing the Main Differences in Growth-Hygiene Factors Among Employees from Public and Private Hospitals

Analyzing the main differences in growth-hygiene factors among employees from public and private hospitals, the empirical results of Mann-Whitney revealed statistical differences among employees for: having a listener of ideas, receiving encouragement when setting goals, receiving training for the tasks, receiving the necessary information to perform the work tasks and being motivated by management, line manager, co-workers and job itself (Table 2.3).

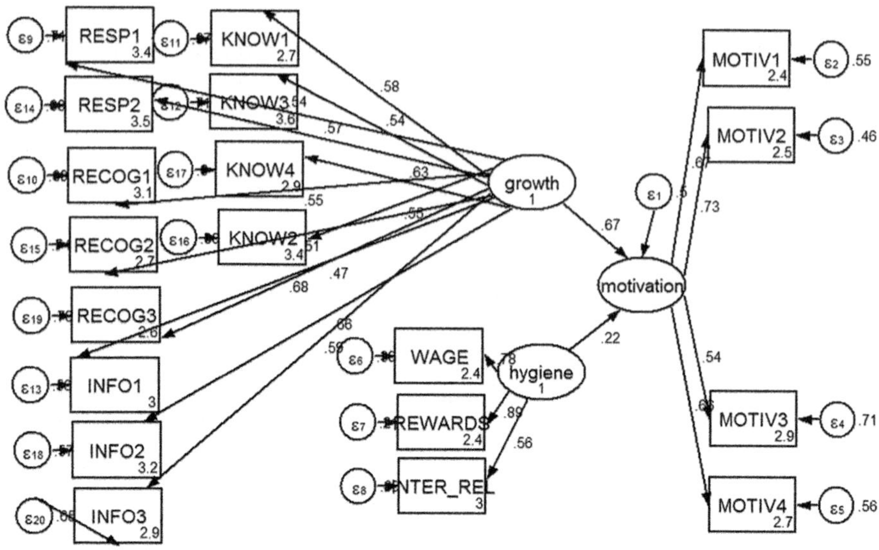

Fig. 2.2 The structural model of employees' motivation in Jordanian hospitals

It is interesting to mention that there are not statistical differences between the opinions of employees from the public and private hospitals regarding extrinsic factors such as wage, rewards or interpersonal relations, highlighting that not financial incentives are the main reason for the decision of people to work in a private hospital.

Regarding the growth factors of having a listener of the ideas, thoughts and suggestions (Recog.2), receiving encouragement when setting goals (Recog.3) and receiving training for the tasks (Know.1), employees declared that they have perceived a higher level of motivation in private hospitals comparative to public ones. Instead, for the factor of receiving the necessary information to perform work tasks, employees from public hospitals perceived a higher level of motivation.

Regarding the main sources of motivation, there are also statistical differences between the opinions of employees from private and public hospitals, revealing that the employees from private hospitals are more motivated by management, manager, co-workers and job itself than the ones from public hospitals.

2.5 Discussion and Conclusions

The objective of this study was to identify the main motivational factors for the employees from Jordanian private and public hospitals to see what kind of factors will manifest a higher impact on the overall level of motivation. Also, the paper aimed to analyze the potential differences in the opinions of employees from public

Table 2.3 The main results of Mann-Whitney test

	Mann-Whitney U	Wilcoxon W	Z	Asymp. Sig. (two tailed)
Wage level	11,773.000	35,426.000	−0.070	0.944
Rewards	11,657.000	35,310.000	−0.220	0.826
"Meeting new people"	11,661.000	17,656.000	−0.217	0.829
Responsibility	11,568.500	35,221.500	−0.354	0.723
Knowledge to make own decisions	11,276.000	17,271.000	−0.751	0.453
Recognition 1—communicate ideas, thoughts and suggestions about the job	11,492.000	17,487.000	−0.441	0.659
Recognition 2—having a ready listener for ideas, thoughts and suggestions	9836.000	33,489.000	−2.591	**0.010**
Recognition 3—receiving encouragement when setting goals	9747.000	33,400.000	−2.695	**0.007**
Knowledge 1—receiving training for work tasks	10,527.000	34,180.000	−1.682	**0.093**
Knowledge 2—having the necessary skills to perform work tasks	11,182.000	17,177.000	−0.873	0.383
Knowledge 3—having the knowledge needed to make the decisions	11,373.500	17,368.500	−0.615	0.538
Knowledge 4—receiving vocational education at the place of work	11,212.000	17,207.000	−0.798	0.425
Information 1—the company has a well-defined mission statement?	11,660.500	35,313.500	−0.216	0.829
Information 2—receiving the necessary information to perform the work tasks	10,542.000	16,537.000	−1.682	**0.093**
Information 3—having knowledge regarding the company (e.g. objectives, visions)	11,800.500	35,453.500	−0.034	0.973
Motivation 1—feeling motivated by management?	10,380.000	34,033.000	−1.863	**0.062**
Motivation 2—feeling motivated by the line manager?	9543.500	33,196.500	−2.951	**0.003**
Motivation 3—feeling motivated by the co-workers?	9974.000	33,627.000	−2.432	**0.015**
Motivation 4—feeling motivated by performing the job (i.e. the job itself)?	9854.500	33,507.500	−2.567	**0.010**

This table presents the empirical results of Mann-Whitney test pointing out the main differences of perceptions related to growth-hygiene factors by type of hospital
Bold figures highlighted the statistical significant relationships for a significance level of 10%
[a]Grouping variable: Type of hospital

vs. private hospitals regarding the main growth and hygiene motivational factors. A structural equation model tested the Herzberg's two-factor theory of work motivation empirically. This study was based on a sample of 325 employees from 6 hospitals in Jordan.

The findings of research support the two-factor theory of work motivation, revealing that both hygiene and growth motivation factors manifest a positive impact on the overall degree of motivation.

The empirical results revealed that growth factors manifested a higher impact on the overall level of motivation comparative with the hygiene factors, but both of them generate an increasing level of motivation. Regarding the hygiene factors, rewards have a higher impact on motivation, this further revealing the importance of monetary rewards in work motivation.

The well-defined mission statement of the company, having the necessary information for performing tasks, and receiving vocational education at the workplace are considered to be the growth factors with a highest impact on overall motivation of employees. Therefore, knowledge and information had the greatest effect on work motivation, while feedback and responsibility had a lesser impact on work motivation.

Analyzing the differences between employees from private and public hospitals regarding the main motivational factors, it is worth to mention that there are not statistical differences between the opinions of employees from public and private hospitals regarding wage, rewards or interpersonal relations, highlighting that not financial incentives are the main reason for the decision of people to work in a private hospital.

But regarding the growth factors, employees from private hospitals in Jordan declared to be more motivated by having a listener of their ideas, thoughts and suggestions, by receiving encouragement or receiving training for their tasks.

This implies that in order to get motivated employees, management needs to give their employees knowledge, information and training. By creating such a context, the intrinsic value of employees is likely to improve, and they will be able to advance in their occupational role.

References

AbuAlRub, R. F., & Al-Zaru, I. M. (2008). Job stress, recognition, job performance and intention to stay at work among Jordanian hospital nurses. *Journal of Nursing Management, 16*(3), 227–236.

AbuAlRub, R. F., Omari, F. H., & Al-Zaru, I. M. (2009). Support, satisfaction and retention among Jordanian nurses in private and public hospitals. *International Nursing Review, 56*(3), 326–332.

AbuAlRub, R. F. (2010). Work and non-work social support and intent to stay at work among Jordanian hospital nurses. *International Nursing Review, 57*(2), 195–201.

Al-Faouri, I., Al-Ali, N., & Al-Shorman, B. (2014). The influence of emotional intelligence training on nurses? Job satisfaction among Jordanian nurses. *European Journal of Scientific Research, 117*(4), 486–494.

Band, G., Shah, N. V., Sriram, R., Appliances, E. (2016, September). Herzberg two factor theory among the management faculty in Nagpur city. In *International Conference on Management and Information Systems* (Vol. 23, p. 24).

Franco, L. M., Bennett, S., Kanfer, R., & Stubblebine, P. (2004). Determinants and consequences of health worker motivation in hospitals in Jordan and Georgia. *Social Science Medicine, 58*(2), 343–355.

Herzberg, F. (1971). *Work and the nature of man.* New York: World Publishing.

Herzberg, F., Mausner, B., & Bloch Snyderman, B. (2005). *The motivation to work.* Piscataway, NJ: Transaction Publishers.

Kontodimopoulos, N., Paleologou, V., & Niakas, D. (2009). Identifying important motivational factors for professionals in Greek hospitals. *BMC Health Services Research, 9*(1), 1.

Lambrou, P., Kontodimopoulos, N., & Niakas, D. (2010). Motivation and job satisfaction among medical and nursing staff in a Cyprus public general hospital. *Human Resources for Health, 8*(1), 1.

Lo, L. Y. S., Lin, S. W., & Hsu, L. Y. (2016). Motivation for online impulse buying: A two-factor theory perspective. *International Journal of Information Management, 36*(5), 759–772.

Lundberg, C., Gudmundson, A., & Andersson, T. D. (2009). Herzberg's two-factor theory of work motivation tested empirically on seasonal workers in hospitality and tourism. *Tourism Management, 30*(6), 890–899.

Mrayyan, M. T. (2005). Nurse job satisfaction and retention: comparing public to private hospitals in Jordan. *Journal of Nursing Management, 13*(1), 40–50.

Mrayyan, M. T. (2008). Predictors of hospitals' organizational climates and nurses' intent to stay in Jordanian hospitals. *Journal of Research in Nursing, 13*(3), 220–233.

Mrayyan, M., & Al-Faouri, I. (2008). Nurses' career commitment and job performance: Differences across hospitals. *Nursing Leadership, 21*(2), 101–117.

Muslim, N. A., Dean, D., & Cohen, D. (2016). Employee job search motivation factors: An evidence from electricity provider company in Malaysia. *Procedia Economics and Finance, 35*, 532–540.

Ruthankoon, R., & Olu Ogunlana, S. (2003). Testing Herzberg's two-factor theory in the Thai construction industry. *Engineering, Construction and Architectural Management, 10*(5), 333–341.

Saleh, A., Darawad, M., & Al-Hussami, M. (2014). Organizational commitment and work satisfaction among Jordanian nurses: A comparative study. *Life Science Journal, 11*(2), 31–36.

Sanjeev, M. A., & Surya, A. V. (2016). Two factor theory of motivation and satisfaction: An empirical verification. *Annals of Data Science, 3*(2), 155–173.

Schneider, F., Buehn, A., & Montenegro, C. (2010). *Shadow economies all over the world: New estimates for 162 countries from 1999 to 2007.* Discussion Paper. World Bank.

Singer, M. F. (2016). *A quantitative study of job satisfaction as it relates to educational level of law enforcement officers*. Scottsdale, AZ: Northcentral University.

*** Stata 13 Software.

Chapter 3
Assessment of Employments: An Essential Process in Increasing the Efficiency of Human Capital Use Within the Romanian Health-Care Facilities

Cătălina Oana Mirică (Dumitrescu)

Abstract The labor management process in an organization shall decisively determine its success, the involvement of the management in the employments' assessment process, and the increase of the organization's efficiency by clearly defining the role and importance of each employment in the organizational chart. In the Romanian health system, the employments' assessment process has a limitative character and, for the most part, is strictly applied in order to determine the amount of wage, the real value of this process being substantially reduced, and the issues related to the importance and value being largely ignored. The typology of used methodologies and the manner in which they are applied may guide the organization to success. That is why, the preoccupation in increasing the efficiency of the employments' assessment process should be a reference point within organizations with specific activity in the field of health. The prepared study points out the issue of the reduced importance attached to the employments' assessment process in particular and is based on an analysis of internal regulations of some health-care facilities in Romania and the provisions enunciated on the tackled problems. The clarity and equilibrium of the provisions on the employments' assessment process determines the manner in which they shall be effectively applied at a later period, the elimination of the subjectivism of this process as far as possible, and the quotation of the respective employment at the declared value.

Keywords Management • Assessment process • Employment • Regulation • Recruitment • Promotion • Waging • Performance

---

C.O. Mirică (Dumitrescu) (✉)
Management Collage at Bucharest University of Economic Studies, Bucharest, Romania
e-mail: catalina.dumitrescu26@yahoo.com

S. Văduva et al. (eds.), *Solutions for Business, Culture and Religion in Eastern Europe and Beyond*, DOI 10.1007/978-3-319-63369-5_3

3.1 Introduction

The purpose of this article is to inform as many people as possible about the current status of the medical staff in Romania and to present both the theoretical and the practical elements that lead to the development of the assessment process of employees within the Romanian health-care facilities. The desire to thoroughly study this theme is older, the topic having always been of interest for both the author and his family. Based on official and sometimes unofficial sources, the status of many health-care facilities and their problems are already known. The most important fact is that, over time, we did not succeed in finding the arguments according to which the medical staff (but also the auxiliary personnel), having a very advanced education in this field and proving much professionalism in the relationship with patients, is lacking the smile of fulfillment and accomplishment.

The assessment of employments in Romania within health-care facilities is a real issue, and that is why this author considers that our country should follow the footsteps of some developed states but with the necessary adaptations regarding the psychological and economical profile of our country.

Certainly, the process is quite difficult but not impossible. This is because our country and, implicitly, its health-care facilities are facing a lot of problems such as the insufficient budget allocated annually, bad management, mass-media campaigns that denigrate doctors, the more and more precarious health of the Romanian people, the colossal businesses of the pharmaceutical industry, as well as many other elements that provide us with an alarming landscape regarding the condition of the Romanian medical worker.

Whatever the field of activity be, the Romanian people are well known for their ability to learn and adapt, and that is why a very great demand of Romanian workforce still exists on the foreign medical market. For this reason, we must give merit to this country and its health-care facilities, by appreciating the quality of work that they carry on and, of course, by salary motivation.

3.2 Literature

The assessment of employment is a **comparative** process because it involves relationships and not absolute values; it is a process of **judgment** because it relies on the interpretation of information about employments (information collected with the aid of job analysis questionnaires), on the comparison of employments, and on the development of a structure of gradation; it is an **analytical** process because the appreciations being made are documented by collecting data; it is a **structural** process because it relies on a pattern allowing assessors to judge rationally and consistently (Deaconu, Lefter, & Manolescu, 2012, p. 76). The assessment of employments refers to the assessment of relative requirements of various employments within an organization. Its common purpose is to provide a basis for the correlation of differences of payment levels with various requirements of the job. So, it is an instrument, which may be used in determining a payment structure (Torrington, Hall, & Taylor, 2005, p. 619). The assessment of employments involves, on the one hand, the determination of the importance of that job in relation to other jobs from the same trade or speciality and, on the other, the determination of the importance of that job in relation to the position from different trades or specialities (Pitaru, 2006, p. 167).

A very important problem related to the payment of personnel salaries is the assessment of employments due to the fact that the employment is a fundamental component or working mechanism or instrument used in the elaboration of salary systems. The assessment of employments is a procedure used in order to determine hierarchies, not only in the sphere of jobs, but also in the sphere of salaries, the assessment being a stage preliminary to the determination of salaries in regard to the requests or requirements of non-vacancies (Manolescu, Lefter, & Deaconu, 2007, p. 531). The main reason for introducing of the assessments of employments is to provide the correctness in the payment policy and to increase the feeling of employees that they are treated correctly. Also, it is used as an instrument in the restructuring of the organization and in harmonizing the terms and conditions afferent to various groups of employees.

The determination of the level or the relative importance of each and every factor within the employment shall finally define the quotation of that employment. Therefore, the development and implementation of this system of assessment factors, which would allow the placement of each and every job of value level in the hierarchy of the organization's jobs, appear as being necessary (Manolescu & Viorel, 1995, p. 276). Such assessment systems are based on the use and combination of varied assessment methods: method of dots, method of comparing factors, method of classification, and method of setting the hierarchy.

3.3 Methods, Study, and Results

This study used a questionnaire in order to find out personal and professional information about employees, in order to carry out a more comprehensive research at a later period and to perform an assessment of employments similar to other European developed countries. The majority of questions were closed questions. The reason for choosing this method was to help the medical personnel be relaxed and for them to answer sincerely the questions presented in the questionnaire. The observation was accompanied by informal discussions centered on the complaints, issues, and difficulties that employees encounter in their activity.

The study presented in this paperwork was completed in 2015. The methodology used for the collection of data/answers was a questionnaire given to the medical staff and the auxiliary personnel in three Romanian hospitals, namely, Sfantul Pantelimon Clinical Emergency Hospital, Floreasca Clinical Emergency Hospital, and Sanador Hospital. All three hospitals analyzed are well-established facilities in training and

Table 3.1 The structure of human resources based on the level of studies

Level of studies	Higher education	Short-term higher education	Secondary education	Post-secondary education	Total
No. of persons: Hospital Sfantul Pantelimon	863	6	270	414	1553
No. of persons: Hospital Floreasca	1708	4	398	964	3074
No. of persons: Sanador hospital	268	10	106	344	728
Total	2839	20	774	1722	5355

Source: Database of hospitals 2015

Table 3.2 The structure of human resources based on the category of personnel

Category of personnel	Medical personnel	Nonmedical personnel	Total
No. of persons: Hospital Sfantul Pantelimon	1461	92	1553
No. of persons: Hospital Floreasca	2811	263	3074
No. of persons: Sanador hospital	658	7	728
Total	4930	425	5355

Source: Database of hospitals 2015

promoting specialists of high professional standing, which rely on recognized professional criteria of prophylaxis, diagnostic, treatment, and management.

Currently, based on the job title list, **5355 employees** carry on their activity within these three hospitals. The structure of personnel employed may be detailed based on more criteria in the following way (Table 3.1).

The weight of higher education personnel is the heaviest in the structure of three hospitals, more precisely about 49%; the post-secondary education personnel represents approximately 35%, in this category being included junior nurses and a great part of the auxiliary personnel of hospitals; the secondary education personnel represents approximately 15%; and, last but not least, the category of personnel with the lightest weight is represented by short-term higher education personnel—1%.

From the vocational training point of view, it may be observed that in the case of *Sfantul Pantelimon* and *Floreasca* hospitals, approximately half of the total personnel employed (both hospitals having 56%) is represented by higher education personnel, which may lead to a higher quality of vocational education and activity carried on by the personnel concerned (Table 3.2 and Fig. 3.1).

Based on the category of personnel, considering the field of activity, 91.66% of all personnel working in the three hospitals are medical personnel, this category including doctors, residents, and auxiliary medical personnel, and the weight of nonmedical personnel is 8.33%. For all three hospitals analyzed, the weight of medical personnel exceeds 90% of all employees (Table 3.3).

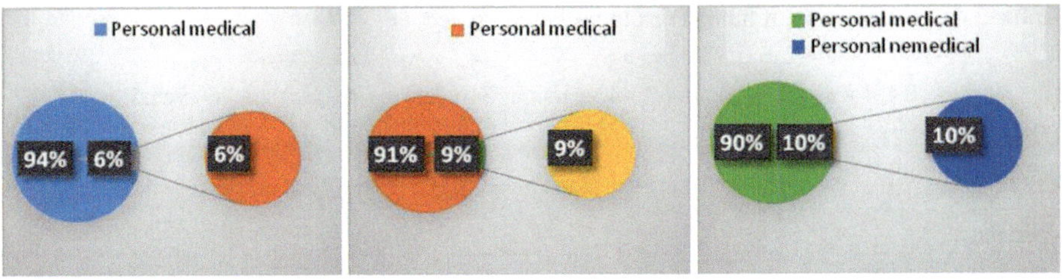

Fig. 3.1 Category of personnel. Source: Database of hospitals 2015

Table 3.3 The structure of human resources based on sex

Category of personnel	Number of employees	Weight
"Sf. Pantelimon hospital"		
Men	356	23%
Women	1197	77%
Total	**1553**	**100%**
"Floreasca hospital"		
Men	**736**	**24%**
Women	**2338**	**76%**
Total	**3074**	**100%**
"Sanador hospital"		
Men	206	28%
Women	522	72%
Total	**728**	**100%**

Source: Database of hospitals 2015

Of the total 5355 employees existing within the three hospitals, over 72% are women, and men represent the rest. In other words, more than three quarters of employees are women. This finding is valid for each facility analyzed, the weight of women in the total employees being approximately 70% (Table 3.4).

The age group mostly encountered within employees is comprised between 25 and 34 years old (about 50%), a thing that is easy to explain because all residents of public hospitals are included in this age group. At the opposite end, fewer persons are over 64 years old. Currently, consultants, senior consultants, and one CMF professor with the age above this limit can be found in each hospital.

Of the total of 286 persons interviewed, the mostly encountered age average is comprised between 46 and 55 years old (33%), and 31% are 36–45 years old; the medical personnel with the age between 26 and 35 years old (26%), between 0 and 25 years old (7%), and over 65 years old (3%) is mostly represented by resident doctors.

Based on the assessment of the results in the questionnaires, it turns out that 65% of the medical personnel is represented by women and 35% by men. Women have a quite high percentage compared to men. Of the total of respondents interviewed, it shows that 65.66% of them are married, and the rest of 34.33% are not married. The

Table 3.4 The structure of human resources based on age

Age	0–24 years old	25–34 years old	35–44 years old	45–54 years old	55–64 years old	Over 64 years old	Total
Sf. Pantelimon hospital							
No. of persons	38	630	547	226	107	5	1553
Hospital Floreasca							
No. of persons	48	1594	933	344	149	6	3074
Sanador hospital							
No. of persons	23	245	206	143	106	5	728
Total	109	2469	1686	713	362	16	5355

Source: Database of hospitals 2015

majority of unmarried employees are between 20 and 35 years old; most are new graduates, currently resident doctors. There are exceptions of unmarried people over 40 years old. Within the three hospitals, 74.33% are doctors, 16.66% are resident doctors, and 9% are nurses. As it may be observed in the above graphs, the heaviest weight of 95% doctors is represented by the Sanador Hospital, while Sf. Pantelimon and Floreasca hospitals have in "custody" resident doctors but also have a relatively good percentage of nurses in comparison with the Sanador private hospital.

The question "Do you think your employment is safe?" refers to the safety of the employment. Fifty-eight percent of the respondents say that they have a feeling of safety in connection with the position they are occupying, but this time the percentage is superior in the public hospitals. We can surmise that the public hospitals have a higher percent not only because they are financed by the state budget and, therefore, they enter into the category of public institutions but also because 68% of their employees have an accumulated service of over 10 years, and those that fulfill this condition have a permanent employment within hospitals.

Fifty-nine percent of the respondents stated that they are not happy with their own career within the hospital.

The reason for this result, especially in the case of the Sf. Pantelimon and Floreasca hospitals, is because the majority included in this category are resident doctors, which consider that the development of the doctor profession is a weakness due to the very long time that lapses until they reach the pinnacle of their profession, by comparison to other jobs. Conversely, in the case of private hospitals, the situation is opposite, especially if we refer to the Sanador Hospital, where the personnel is periodically assisted with professional growth by attending training courses in Italy, within the hospitals of Sanador Group. Also, they have the possibility to develop their own career in these hospitals, this representing the reason for which 64% of the total of personnel interviewed within the gynecology department have a positive mention on the professional status.

The majority of members of the medical community show certain symptoms that may obstruct their medical activity, 66% of those claiming that health issues are affecting their professional duties (tasks). We observe that the personnel analyzed claims that these heath issues influence their professional efficiency, mainly for the Sf. Pantelimon Hospital (75%) and the Floreasca Hospital (69%).

Also, 57% of the total of persons interviewed purport that they have frequently signs of accentuated tiredness and partial losses of the working capacity, issues due, first of all, to working conditions. We find the personnel of Sf. Pantelimon Hospital as being the eloquent example for this situation, because over 68% of its employees show these negative symptoms that may reflect on the efficiency of their activity. At the same time, as results from the analysis, the less-affected employees by the working conditions are those of the Sanador Hospital (47%).

The salary represents a primary factor in the choices that employees within the hospital make in regard to their own employment. Being asked if the income derived from the medical activity is enough in order to provide the family existence, 56% of the sample members claim that the salary is insufficient for providing for their family. At this question, the answers of the respondents were at opposite ends. More precisely, if within the private hospital (Sanador 71%) the personnel considers that the income obtained is a motivating one, in the case of public hospitals (Sf. Pantelimon 23% and Floreasca 38%), the situation is totally different, with more than half of the total employees not considering that the income obtained may help them cover their daily life.

3.4 Conclusions

Starting from the proven fact that the importance of increasing the efficiency of the economic activity brings together issues regarding innovation and modernization, the human resource problem is also a defining one included in this trend. That is why the pattern-making and rethinking of employment in a direct correlation with the results obtained by individuals in their respective positions is the essential issue pertaining to the development of service activity, mainly in the medical field and, in the present instance, in Romania.

This study highlighted complex problems related both to the conceptual and the applicative issue of the questions addressed. In the majority of cases, the periodical assessment of employment is not an essential issue; most employers believe that if an employee is thought good from the beginning, further problems cannot emerge. This issue is especially related to the mentality in the system, to the vocational training of the manager, and to the direct awareness of the role of assessment in the process of increasing the efficiency of the hospitals' activity. Rapid and direct solutions for improving the existing situation refer to issues concerning the manager's activity, the change of the manner based on which he/she addresses the questions by attending training courses specialized in the medical field, and the repositioning in his/her system of managerial values of the importance of employments' assessment.

Also, by organizing symposiums and training courses specialized in this issue, the possibility of direct interaction between organizations having the same medical specificity is developed, experiences are being shared, and the correction of some errors is made by learning from positive examples.

References

Deaconu, A., Lefter, V., & Manolescu, A. (2012). *Human resource management.* Bucharest, Romania: Edition Prouniversitaria.

Manolescu, A., & Viorel, L. (1995). *Human resource management.* Bucharest, Romania: Edition Didactic and Pedagogical.

Manolescu, A., Viorel, L., & Alecxandrina, D. (Eds.). (2007). Maria Moldovan-Scholz, Cristian.

Marinaş, E. N., Irinel, M., & Ramona, P. (2007). *Human resource management.* Bucharest, Romania: Edition Economic.

Pitaru, D. H. (2006). *Designing job descriptions, evaluation of jobs and employees.* Bucharest, Romania: Irecson.

Torrington, D., Hall, L., & Taylor, S. (2005). *Human resource management* (6th ed.). Upper Saddle River, NJ: Pearson Education.

Websites

http://legislatiamuncii.manager.ro/a/2124/evaluarea-posturilor.html
http://urgentapantelimon.ro/
http://www.haygroup.com/ro/services/index.aspx?id=5785
http://www.scub.ro/
https://www.sanador.ro/

Chapter 4
The Impact of Cross-Border Cooperation on Human Resources Employed in Local Administration: The Case of the Romanian-Hungarian Border Area

Daniel Badulescu and Ramona Simut

Abstract Local communities in border areas, which have been until recently separated by political borders intended to legitimate and defend the essence of the nation-state, discovered in cross-border cooperation (CBC) a facilitator of good neighborly relations, economic opportunities, or a possibility to promote innovative and high-quality public services. At a European level, cross-border cooperation, supported by the integration policies of the EU, highlighted the growing role of local authorities and communities, as stakeholders and beneficiaries alike. This paper presents the results of a survey-based research conducted among managers, experts, and staff from local public administration, across the Hungarian-Romanian border, analyzing their opinion regarding the changes to their institutions brought forth by their involvement in cross-border actions in the Bihor–Hajdú-Bihar Euroregion. It focuses on revealing aspects such as the issue of human resources in local administration, the relationship between CBC projects developed by local administration and the employees' expectations, involvement in decision-making, and prospects and career satisfaction in (local) public administration. Research results show that the local governments' involvement in CBC projects should not only consider the opportunities of additional financing sources or improving cross-border relations in various fields (economic, cultural, communication, health, public order, tourism), as the results also reveal specific vulnerabilities and a particular indifference of local administration staff to generous, but often less tangible, objectives of CBC projects. The research also highlights the key role of human resource quality, echoing the role of managers in the selection, retention, and efficient use of human resources, linking the projects' objectives to individual performance and expectations of a career in public administration.

Keywords Romania-Hungary cross-border cooperation • Human resources • Local public administration

D. Badulescu, Ph.D. (✉) • R. Simut, Ph.D.
Faculty of Economic Sciences, University of Oradea, Oradea, Romania
e-mail: dbadulescu@uoradea.ro; simut.ramona@yahoo.com

S. Văduva et al. (eds.), *Solutions for Business, Culture and Religion in Eastern Europe and Beyond*, DOI 10.1007/978-3-319-63369-5_4

4.1 Introduction

The study of cross-border cooperation reveals a high complexity of forms and consequences on a political, administrative, economic, and social level. It represents a meeting point between the specific context of each cross-border relation (historically, economically, politically, and socially determined) on one hand and the dimension and aspirations of local actors, policies, and objectives of increasing European integration, on the other hand. In light of these various contributions, CBC goes beyond the immediate and palpable scope of improving relationships between people and organizations on both sides of the border. Cross-border cooperation refers to identifying common issues, responding to social needs, improving everyday life, mitigating the consequences arising from the administration of different national territories (different legal, social, or cultural systems), increasing the attractiveness and competitiveness of the regions, and stimulating and inspiring stakeholders in common action beyond national borders. In this paper we explore the issue of cross-border cooperation's impact on human resources from local administration, through a number of key research elements: strengths and weaknesses of local public administration, expectations and results of organizational change, CBC's role on public administration reform and modernization, employees' opinion on the usefulness and effectiveness of CBC projects, and the importance of a career in local public government.

The paper is organized as follows: after some introductory consideration, we review several theoretical considerations on the (European) cross-border cooperation and the role of local authorities and their capabilities in order to implement valuable CBC programs. We focus on the Hungary-Romania cross-border cooperation, especially on the Bihor–Hajdú-Bihar Euroregion. In the second part of the paper, we approach the survey-based research performed, presenting and discussing the results, and in the final part, we draw conclusions.

4.2 The Emergence and Development of Cross-Border Cooperation

The theoretical foundations of CBC are claimed from several sources. Some of them stem from the *new economic geography and the core-periphery model*, (Krugman, 1991; Venables, 1996; Krugman & Venables, 1995; Baldwin & Forslid, 2000), or cross-border regionalism (Scott, 1999). Others originate from border studies, based on its symbolism and consequences, "a particular type of obstacle which restricts or impedes the smooth transfer or free movement of a person or commodity from one place to another" (Nijkamp & Batten, 1990), with a purpose derived from the state's functions (Knippenberg & Markusse, 1999, pp. 1–10), defending and legitimizing the territory of the nation-state and outlining their extreme limits (Brunet-Jailly, 2005, p. 636). Borders act, therefore, as an obstacle to cooperation, based on the existence of significant legal, political, economic, or cultural differences (Anderson & Bort, 2001), a consequence of its political and military function, designed rather to separate than to connect and to indicate the distance to the state's center of decision (Martinez, 1994; Gasparini, 2008).

The first forms of cross-border cooperation originated in the late 1950s in Dutch-German border regions (1958), the Franco-German-Swiss Upper Rhine region (1963), and the Franco-German-Luxembourg border region (1968). It is no coincidence that the area of such early cooperation (and the time period) coincides with the formation of the Common Market (1957) and the reconciliation processes between states that, in the first half of the twentieth century, were engaged in deep political and military conflicts, (European Commission, 2015). We should not ignore the fact that CBC forms also developed in independent frameworks (or just influenced by European integration), boosted by bilateral relations between states and the strength, ambition, and competence (autonomy) of local communities.

The unprecedented political, economic, and diplomatic transformations occurring in Europe during the late 1980s and early 1990s had dramatic consequences, noticeable up to this day. These transformations were a condition for the development of a European identity, yet they generated contradictions and divisiveness; they redefined the perception of "we" and "others" or "inside" and "outside" of the EU (border), the EU integration process "melting" the internal frontiers of the EU but "freezing" the external frontiers (Topaloglou, Kallioras, Manetos, & Petrakos, 2005).

Guided by a broader view of the European integration, which exceeded the limited framework promoted by the member states, the EEC and then the EU have undertaken CBC programs since the early 1990s, through a series of tools and support programs for CBC. INTERREG —established in 1990 through financial support—was instrumental in strengthening local cooperation. Since 1997, its role has extended to cooperation frameworks in areas covering regions from many countries and, subsequently, after 2006, adds the geopolitical dimension (the Baltic Sea, the Danube, the Adriatic, and the Alps). In parallel, a legal tool for territorial cooperation was established—the European Grouping of Territorial Cooperation (EGTC) in 2007.

This proves that territorial cooperation has diversified and neighborhood approaches have become more complex (European Commission, 2015). Today, as Perkmann (2003) noted more than 10 years ago, "there are virtually no local or regional authorities in border areas that are not somehow involved in cross-border co-operation" (Perkmann, 2003, p. 2), creating a large network of cooperation and Euroregions, an image of a borderless Europe, "a Europe of the Regions, rather than the Europe of the Nations" (Medeiros, 2011, p. 2). According to the Association of European Border Regions (AEBR) in 2016, there were 178 cross-border regions and 23 European Groupings of Territorial Cooperation (AEBR, 2016); meanwhile the European Committee of the Regions (2016) (EU-appointed authority in relation with EGTCs) counts, at the end of 2016, 63 EGTCs entities and 17 large-scale cross-border cooperations. The purpose of their existence is ensuring reasonable economic efficiency, the capacity to attain common social and cultural objectives and needs to render CBC comprehensive, to allow and stimulate the organizing of common activities, to include as many daily life aspects in border areas—economy, employment, leisure, culture, social issues, housing, planning, and so on—and to engage cross-border partners and stakeholders, in all areas, on all societal and economic levels: national, regional, and local (AEBR, 2000).

In spite of such generous objectives, there are numerous situations when CBC was interpreted individually or opportunistically: border regions first develop their own projects and priorities, independent of one another, and then contact partners on the other side of the border, in order to involve them as well, transforming the annexes of national plans into cross-border programs and projects. Some local entities participated in CBC programs mostly in order to obtain (EU) funding, necessary for the financing of investment projects, irrespective of economic, social, or civil security reasons. In other cases, cross-border cooperation was artificial, formal, "cooperation for the sake of cooperation" (Badulescu, Kolozsi, Badulescu, & Lupau, 2016). Cross-border cooperation should not take place only due to the availability of external funding, even if such funding is an important stimulus and catalyst of cooperation.

4.3 Local Authorities and Cross-Border Cooperation

According to Svensson (2015), local authorities are considered to be "the backbone of CBC cooperation," the most important and the nearest institutional actor for border communities (I.S.I.G., 2013). In addition, local authorities participate themselves in high numbers in CBC projects, entering a tough competition to access additional funding. In one of the few studies dedicated to the comparative analysis of human resources in border regions' public administration, Abrudan, Săveanu, Matei, and Ujhelyi (2015) approached the implementation of new public management principles in local public administration institutions in Bihor County (Romania) and Hajdú-Bihar County (Hungary). They found some differences in the perception of Romanian and Hungarian employees in local public administration institutions; however they mentioned specific autonomy and flexibility characterizing their work, a significant involvement of subordinates in the decisional process, and an interest of managers to retain and improve, through trust and cooperation, their relations with the employees.

One of the main vulnerabilities of CBC is its poor institutionalization, which affects medium- and short-term projects. Consequently, this situation is not favorable to the creation of a valuable human and social capital and of a sufficient number of qualified personnel in CBC-specific activities. In public administration institutions, even if people employed in CBC projects enjoy certain job stability and career prospects as civil servants (Badulescu, Hoffman, Badulescu, & Simut, 2016), their transition from one position to another and the inconsistency of certain tasks and objectives can negatively affect the "organization's commitment or experience of cross-border cooperation" (O'Dowd, McCall, & Damkat, 2006, p. 16). Lepik (2009) gives a warning about the difficulty of attracting and qualified staff (…) if the completion of some European programs requires a large volume of work and remarkable administrative abilities. Describing the shortcomings of the cooperation of local authorities on the USA-Mexico border, Saint-Germain (1995) points out that cooperation between managers of public institutions on both sides of the frontier is and remains essential for the generation of common and flexible solutions and in order to maintain local autonomy. The centralization of such decisions is undesirable and inefficient, as it "will only further erode the local managers' already weakened abilities to make decisions on matters that directly affect them" (Saint-Germain 1995, p. 514).

Addressing PHARE CBC partnership development, Szmigiel-Rawska (2016) highlights the importance of workplace stability, which is itself conditioned by the accumulation and internalization of knowledge acquired by individual employees in the organization. Moreover, local administration should take into consideration that accomplishing their objectives is additionally influenced by the efficiency of managing the internal and external relations of the organization and of the joint involvement of politicians and civil servants. It depends on the local government managers that these interactions lead to the "creation of effective cooperation mechanisms" and not to distortion and confusion with regard to the purpose and objectives of (local) public institutions. Furthermore, in environment that is less transparent, off-putting, and even hostile to CBC, limited human and financial capacity or political instability can markedly affect the performance of local authorities in CBC (Aston Centre for Europe, 2014, p. 87).

González-Gómez and Gualda (2016) come to the conclusion that, in comparison to other institutional organisms, local governments possess a more flexible structure and representatives who are better suited to develop and optimize cross-border relations, despite limited and often asymmetrical internal competence (González-Gómez & Gualda, 2016, p. 477). The authors also identify the dangers of the implementation of CBC programs: centralized or regional decisions, the disengagement of programs from the day-to-day life of the local inhabitants, and the loss of interest of local actors, who perceive they are living rather at the periphery than a border area.

4.4 Hungary-Romania Cross-Border Cooperation

The border area between Romania and Hungary has considerably benefited from European funds considered for CBC (Feier & Badulescu, 2016). It started off in Romania in 1996, with a pilot cooperation program, followed by in the next year (1997) by the PHARE CBC program. With this, the European Commission extended (for the first time in its history) a program for a border region between two UE candidate countries. Between 1996 and 2003, EU PHARE CBC allocated 34 million euros for projects on the Hungarian side and 28 million for the Romanian side (Regional Office for Cross-border Cooperation for Romanian-Hungarian Border (BRECO, 2015). The next stage of cooperation is represented by HU-RO CBC Program for 2004–2006, with an overall budget of 32 million euros for Hungary

(INTERREG) and 20 million for Romania (PHARE CBC), including national cofinancing (BRECO, 2015).

Since 2007, both Hungary and Romania, as EU member states, can access structural funds as financial support for development, based on the three fundamental objectives: convergence, regional competitiveness and employment, as well as, obviously, European territorial cooperation.

The overall objective of HU-RO CBC 2007–2013 remains unchanged—tightening contacts among communities, economic factors, and people from the border area belonging to the two neighboring countries and aiming at facilitating the common development of the border area while making the most out of the area's comparative advantages to the benefit of both countries. Stimulating cooperation between local administrations is an important part of the new program as the relatively difficult cooperation between Hungarian and Romanian organizations (revealed by previous experiences) is considered as one of the biggest challenges in this partnership. The HU-RO CBC 2007–2013 Program concluded in 2015, benefiting from the $n + 3$ rule, proposed by the European Commission for those countries that fail to finish their projects within the originally proposed time frame (European Commission, 2013). In the final evaluation of the program (BRECO, 2015), 455 projects (out of a total number of 1176 applications) were reported, with 528 beneficiaries/applicants (a project can have more than 1–2 beneficiaries) employing around 201 million EUR (Feier & Badulescu, 2016).

Narrowing down the research to the Bihor–Hajdú-Bihar Euroregion, we realize that this small Euroregion occupies only a quarter of the area, population, and economic potential of the entire HU-RO CBC area. However, the Bihor–Hajdú-Bihar Euroregion registers 185 completed projects (over 40% of the total number of selected projects), using approximately 48% of available funds. Of these 185 projects, we have identified 75 public entities, partners in various cooperation projects, mostly local governments, of which 94 in Romania and 67 in Hungary. It is noted that the county seats—Debrecen (Hungary) and Oradea (Romania)—register about a quarter of the value and the number of approved projects.

4.5 Research Design

The general objective of the empirical research presented in this paper is to evaluate the impact of CBC projects on local administration and, in particular, on human resources employed in these units, i.e., in the components of Bihor–Hajdú-Bihar Euroregion: Hajdú-Bihar County (Hungary) and Bihor County (Romania). The general objective is attained through a number of subthemes of which, relevant to the presented research, we mention: defining the profile of the locality and public administration and the effects of CBC on the reform of public institutions, on the development and consolidation of the human resources' potential, on expectations and results of organizational change, and on career prospects in local public government.

The designed questionnaire consists of 25 questions: 5 single-answer closed questions, 15 multiple-answer closed questions, and 5 multiple choice matrix-type questions. In order to test the survey's reliability, we grouped the questions referring to respondent perceptions and then used Cronbach's alpha method; the alpha coefficient is equal to 0.711, indicating a reliable scale. Eliminating any other item leads to a lower alpha.

According to official documents (National Institute of Statistics (Romania), 2013; Hungarian Central Statistical Office, 2014), in the analyzed area of the HU-RO CBC, namely, Hajdú-Bihar County (Hungary) and Bihor County (Romania), there are 182 local authorities distributed as follows: 62 communes and 19 towns in Hajdú-Bihar County (Hungary) and 91 communes, 4 municipalities, and 6 towns in Bihor County (Romania).

Among these a number of 74 administrative units, which have been involved in at least one project in the HU-RO CBC Programs in the last 10 years, were identified. Of these, 52 are communes: 24 from Hajdú-Bihar and 28 from Bihor; 15 are small towns (under 30,000 inhabitants), 7 from Hajdú-Bihar and 8 from Bihor. The other seven are distributed as follows: one town (over 30,000 inhabitants) in Hajdú-Bihar, two metropolitan areas (Debrecen-HU and Oradea-RO, with over 100,000 inhabitants), and seven regional/county authorities: three from Hajdú-Bihar and four from Bihor.

The questionnaire was sent (by e-mail) to 183 representatives of these 74 units during March–May 2016. A number of 66 responses were received from local/regional administrative units as follows: 42 responses came from villages, 15 from small town, 7 from large town (county seat) and metropolitan area, and, finally, 2 responses from county or regional administrations. In terms of country distribution, a majority of 62% (i.e., 41 responses) come from Romanian administration units, and the rest, 38% (i.e., 25 responses) are from Hungary.

4.6 Results and Discussion

RQ1. The Strengths and Weaknesses of Local Public Administration Management

The strengths of local public administration management are the *flexibility and the promptness* (indicated by ca. 40% of the respondents) both in Romania (28%) and in Hungary (12%). The next strength considered is the *emphasis on quality*, indicated by 29% of the respondents. Regarding the main weaknesses of the management of local government, both Romanian and Hungarian respondents consider the *financial constraints* (indicated by 43% of the respondents) and the *difficulties to employ competent staff* (34%), with minor differences between the two countries. Minor vulnerabilities in the activity of public administration are considered to be *the interference in public administration of outside people* (indicated by 7% of the Hungarian respondents and 4% of the Romanian respondents); meanwhile *the tolerance (or even encouragement) of corruption, favoritism*, and *political clientelism* is considered (surprisingly!) to be nearly nonexistent in the activity of these administrative units. We can notice that, if on national level the differences are insignificant, they appear between units with different characteristics: urban versus rural or even large versus small urban entities. It can be observed that the respondents from most rural communities stated that *flexibility and promptness* represents their strength, with the exception of the respondents from urban areas, who argued that their strength is *the emphasis on quality* (both in Romania and in Hungary). Furthermore, respondents from the institutions located in metropolitan areas consider that *the modern profile, adjusted to European standards*, represents the strength of their institution.

RQ2. The Issue of Human Resources in Local Administration

The issue of recruiting, employing, and retaining human resources in local administration remains critical, due to the crucial role played by the project manager and the key experts in CBC projects. The staff involved in implementing CBC projects have to fulfil several criteria, mainly related to adequate expertise. In order to identify the most important issues in recruiting staff in the analyzed institutions and those working with CBC projects, the following conditions were considered: specialized expertise, informal relations with people in the institution, membership in a political party, and family relationships (Table 4.1).

According to the survey results, 85% of the respondents consider that the most important issue in recruiting staff is *specialized knowledge* (the mean value of responses in the Romanian sample is 3.87, and in the Hungarian sample is 3.92—on a scale from 1, meaning *a very small extent*, to 5, meaning *totally*). On the opposite side, there are the *family relationships*, considered by 88% of respondents as being the most insignificant issue in recruiting (the mean value of responses in the Romanian sample is 1, and in the Hungarian sample is 1.16—on a scale from 1, meaning *a very small extent*, to 5, meaning *totally*). However, when investigating the responses broken down by respondents' location, we find that in the case of large urban towns, *family relationships* are considered by 43% of the respondents as one of the most important issues in personnel recruitment, specialized expertise being assessed as presenting moderate importance (indicated by 57% of the respondents), and *informal relations with people in the institution* and *membership in a political party* are considered not being important for HR recruitment (86% of the respondents). Indeed, there is a significant difference between respondents' opinions by location ($p = 16.58$; sig. = 0.000).

We could assume that the question fulfilled its purpose only to a limited extent, without generating (within the preset answer options) a satisfactory level of sincerity. Local representatives have managed to avoid, likely due to their politically exercised conformism, a direct answer regarding an often unprofessional access to public service. Moreover, these results may be an indicator of the (still) low attraction of the jobs in local administration.

RQ3. CBC Projects and Employees' Expectations

Regarding the extent to which CBC projects corresponded with employees' expectations, we noticed that Romanian respondents consider that CBC projects where

Table 4.1 Relevant factors for recruiting staff in CBC projects

	To a large extent	To a moderate extent	To a very small extent	To a large extent	To a moderate extent	To a very small extent	To a large extent	To a moderate extent	To a very small extent
	Rural communities			Small urban towns			Large towns		
Specialized expertise	86%	14%	0%	100%	0%	0%	43%	57%	0%
Informal relations with people in the institution	7%	26%	67%	0%	27%	73%	0%	14%	86%
Membership in a political party	5%	12%	83%	0%	27%	73%	0%	14%	86%
Family relationship	0%	7%	93%	0%	7%	93%	43%	29%	29%

Source: own calculations, based on the dataset

Table 4.2 The extent to which CBC projects correspond to employee expectations

Country/administrative units		Do not correspond	Corresponding to a limited extent	Corresponding to a significant extent	Total correspondence
RO	Rural communities	17.9%	53.6%	28.6%	0%
	Small urban towns	25.0%	50.0%	25.0%	0%
	Large towns (cities)	25.0%	50.0%	25.0%	0%
	Metropolitan area	0.0%	0.0%	100.0%	0%
HU	Rural communities	14.3%	50.0%	35.7%	0%
	Small urban towns	0.0%	40.0%	60.0%	0%
	Large towns (cities)	0.0%	33.3%	66.7%	0%
	Metropolitan area	0.0%	100.0%	0.0%	0%

Source: own calculations, based on the dataset

their institution has been involved corresponded *to a limited extent* with employee expectations, in most local/regional administrative units. In the case of Hungarian respondents, employee expectations have matched *to a significant extent* with the objectives of the CBC projects implemented by institutions in small urban towns (60%) and large towns (66.7%) but *to a limited extent* in rural communities. The independent sample t-test shows a value of $p = 26.02$ and sig = 0.000, indicating a significant difference between the Romanian respondents and the Hungarian respondents; overall Romanian respondents report that employee expectations *correspond to a limited extent* with the CBC projects, while Hungarian respondents report that the employees' expectations correspond *to a significant extent* with the CBC projects (Table 4.2).

When investigating the perspective of the respondents located in the two metropolitan areas, we noticed that they actually differ, i.e., while in Romania employee expectations matched *to a significant extent* with CBC projects' objectives, in Hungary the match was only to *a limited extent*. However, the limited number of the respondents in this category does not allow us to assume this fundamental change of perspective as being relevant.

RQ4. The Desirability of a Career in Public Service

The survey data indicates that a significant number of respondents would like to work in public service, if they had the opportunity to start a new career/activity. Nevertheless, if we analyze the data on administrative units, we find that the respondents from metropolitan areas were not sure they would choose the same career/activity; meanwhile 50% of Romanian respondents from large towns (cities) stated that they would definitely not continue to work in public service. Meanwhile, all the respondents from Hungarian large towns stated that, most likely, they would continue working in the same field of public services (Table 4.3).

Table 4.3 The career in public administration

Country/administrative units		*If you had the possibility to start a new career/activity, would you still choose to work in public service?* I don't know	Definitely not	Probably not	Probably yes	Definitely yes
RO	Rural communities	3.6%	3.6%	17.9%	64.3%	10.7%
	Small urban towns	25.0%	0.0%	12.5%	50.0%	12.5%
	Large towns (cities)	25.0%	50.0%	0.0%	0.0%	25.0%
	Metropolitan area	100.0%	0.0%	0.0%	0.0%	0.0%
HU	Rural communities	7.1%	21.4%	21.4%	50.0%	0.0%
	Small urban towns	36.3%	0.0%	16.7%	30.3%	16.7%
	Large towns (cities)	0.0%	0.0%	0.0%	100.0%	0.0%
	Metropolitan area	100.0%	0.0%	0.0%	0.0%	0.0%

Source: own calculations, based on the dataset

RQ5. Prospects in Career
The data collected reveals that the largest share of respondents from Romanian and Hungarian public institutions refers to their expectations to work in the same institution, and in the same position, in the following 5 years. Another part of Romanian respondents do not expect to be working in the same institution but in a different job/position, perhaps in another public institution or in the private sector/their own business. These perspectives do not significantly differ from those of Hungarian respondents, which leave room for other possible options yet unspecified (*other cases*).

Both questions are quite general. They do not pursue to assess the current situation but combine anticipation of future options with retrospective attitudes. Except for a few answers coming (perhaps) from those at the end of active life, for most respondents these questions try to find an option and a personal response to key questions such as does there really exist a career in public service? Does a public career provide enough motivations, challenges, and rewards to be considered a viable alternative to other professions and careers in the economy and society?

The survey carried out indicates a moderate attractiveness of local public administration as a career option, also confirmed by several previous researches warning on the difficulties in recruiting and retaining young qualified personnel. Explanations may be found in the different perceptions of managers (as public servants) versus elected representatives, in the on-job stability policies, in the various career alternatives and options (i.e., private sector attractiveness), in the significant urban-rural disparities, etc. A relatively large share of those who want to continue working in the same institution in the future, preferably in the same position, interrelated with the answers to the previous question (the possibility to start a new career) indicating a large part of respondents that would choose local administration jobs, confirms our assessment. This assessment refutes, at least partially, previous research results stating the low attractiveness of the public sector for a successful career or finding that the attractiveness of public service resides in the interest to opportunistically capitalize on the advantages of the jobs in the public sector. Moreover, a clear tendency for continuity in rural and small urban administrative units and (relatively) similar positions, regardless of country, is noticeable.

4.7 Conclusion

Cross-border cooperation is a complex and evolving subject. Even in the relatively small geographic framework of Central and Eastern Europe countries, the diversity and complexity of the phenomenon is obvious. This variety is fueled by the variety of actors and beneficiaries (e.g., local institutions or regional organizations, NGOs, associations, private companies, and citizens), by their experience, capabilities, and ambitions, by the scale of strategies and reforms established at regional or national level, and, not least, by the objectives of European regional integration policies.

Our survey-based research among the Bihor–Hajdú-Bihar Euroregion administrative units revealed several conclusions, as follows:

- Local representatives (both in Romania and Hungary) are quite optimistic, evaluating their institutions as *flexible* and *prompt*, focused on *quality*, and less impaired by the interference of outsiders, by corruption, favoritism, or political clientelism. Their results are negatively influenced by *financial constraints* and the *difficulties in recruiting and employing competent staff*.
- The involvement of local administrative units in cross-border cooperation actions has a limited effect on the reform and modernizing of public administration.
- The issue of recruiting, employing, and retaining human resources remains critical, especially for experts and managers of cross-border projects. However, staff recruitment appears to be done in terms of performance, excluding nepotism, political influence, or informal relations.
- Regarding the extent to which CBC projects corresponded to the employees' expectations, we may see a reticent position of Romanian respondents, contrasting with the (moderate) optimism displayed by Hungarian respondents. The explanations may reside in a more goal-oriented management of Hungarian local governments (confirmed by abovementioned studies) or to Romanian administrations being less experienced in CBC issues.
- A career in public services is indeed a viable option, proven not only by the option of most respondents to start over in the same sector but also by the expectation and intention to work in the same sector, preferably in the same position, in the coming years. A career in public administration provides a sufficient challenge as an alternative to other careers in the economy and society.

Overall, our survey reveals a more complex and less enthusiastic reality than what can be found in the top-down political approaches and public campaigns. It reveals several national differences, but the more obvious seem to be the discrepancies between rural and small urban versus large towns and regional authorities.

The positive impact of cross-border cooperation in solving border problems is not felt with the same intensity in the process of local government modernization nor, especially, in human resources. In comparative terms, it appears that CBC's benefits and utility are better perceived by managers versus other staff or in large urban communities versus rural communities. Moreover, CBC is more realistically and pragmatically capitalized on by Hungarian managers than by their Romanian counterparts.

As a limitation, we have to admit that our study captures and analyzes the managers and staff opinions regarding the transformations generated by the active involvement in cross-border actions only at certain time and in a certain spatial context, i.e., the Hungary-Romania cross-border cooperation. Understanding CBC's effects on human resources in local administration units therefore remains an interesting research area, with substantial theoretical and practical applications. These results could make cross-border cooperation more effective, more genuine, and, not least, most adequate to local communities in border areas.

References

Abrudan, M.-M., Săveanu, T., Matei, M., & Ujhelyi, M. (2015). Obstacles, realities and opportunities in human resources Management in Public Administration Institutions from Bihor County (Romania) and Hajdú-Bihar County (Hungary). *Transylvanian Review of Administrative Sciences, 45*(E), 5–25.

AEBR. (2000). *Practical guide to cross-border cooperation, Third Edition 2000*. Gronau, Germany: Association of European Border Regions (AEBR) and European Commission.

AEBR. (2016). Association of European Border Regions, Regions List. Available from: http://www.aebr.eu/en/members/list_of_members.php (Accessed 2 December 2016).

Anderson, M., & Bort, E. (2001). *The frontiers of the European Union*. Chippenham, UK: Palgrave.

Aston Centre for Europe. (2014). *Local and regional authorities for a successful eastern partnership*. Bruxelles, Belgium: European Union: Committee of the Regions.

Badulescu, A., Kolozsi, L., Badulescu, D., Lupau, C. (2016). Strengths and weaknesses in local public administration in Romania. Preliminary research results. *Proceedings of The 10th International Days of Statistics and Economics*. Prague: University of Economics. September 8–10, 2016.

Badulescu, D., Hoffman, I., Badulescu, A., & Simut, R. (2016). Local authorities' involvement in fostering Hungarian-Romanian cross-border cooperation in tourism. *Lex Localis-Journal of Local Self-Government, 14*(3), 337–358.

Baldwin, R., & Forslid, R. (2000). The Core - periphery model and endogenous growth: Stabilizing and destabilizing integration. *Economica, 67*, 307–324. doi:10.1111/1468-0335.00211.

Brunet-Jailly, E. (2005). Theorizing borders: An interdisciplinary perspective. *Geopolitics, 10*(4), 633–649. doi:10.1080/14650040500318449.

European Commission. (2013). Proposal for a Regulation of the European Parliament and of the Council. Strasbourg, COM (2013) 301 final 2013/0156.

European Commission. (2015). *Territorial Cooperation in Europe. A historical perspective*. Luxembourg: Publications Office of the European Union.

European Committee of the Regions. (2016). European Grouping of Territorial Cooperation, Maps & Register. [Interactiv] Available from: https://portal.cor.europa.eu/egtc/CoRActivities/Pages/egtc-list.aspx (Accessed 12 December 2016).

and choices.[1] Entrepreneurial acting means to work in and with the entrepreneurial functions. This is the role that the entrepreneur gets allocated in the theory of singular economic theories.[2]

"Entrepreneurial functions" means that within the enterprise there are three big blocks, which point out an enterprise as a system of productive potentials. These are the task sectors: system renewing, system use, and system safeguard. Standing behind these task sectors, we can find each entrepreneurial function as visible in the following figure. These are the functions of innovation, coordination, arbitrage, and risk management (Fig. 5.1) (Freiling, 2005, p.142).[3]

The innovation function is a renewing function in the system of entrepreneurial functions. This renewing function always holds the enterprise with its infrastructure on a competitive level and opens the possibility for creating new ideas for the market. The coordination function and the arbitrage function belong as entrepreneurial functions to the mode of system use. The coordination function takes care of what is happening inside the enterprise including the cooperation partners. Internal coordination means product and service production as well as the coordination of the administrative workflow.[4] The arbitrage function doesn't look for the internal processes of the enterprise. This function is only for the external affairs: generating, recognizing, and developing opportunities on the market. These two functions are urgently necessary to lead an enterprise.[5] Risk management means to make the system safe and to judge about risk assumption and diversification of risks.[6]

With this, there is an abstraction from the person of the entrepreneur. So, an entrepreneur is everybody acting in the entrepreneurial functions. But, there remains the question *who* it is, who is acting in the entrepreneurial functions. Because enterprises are not governed by themselves, they are also not acting alone.

Obviously, the individual entrepreneurial abilities play a role in the market process. And this "acting in the entrepreneurial functions" as an all-including term doesn't automatically give success for an enterprise. Entrepreneurial functions without thinking and acting human behind them, are not thinkable. And so, the necessity comes out that there is a person who needs cognition as a precondition for entrepreneurial acting.

Information is necessary for the cognition bringing out entrepreneurial acting on a basis of knowledge. The entrepreneur needs information from his enterprise, but also from outside for acting well in the entrepreneurial functions. Information and knowledge grow from perception. And, because the entrepreneur is a human, his entrepreneurial ability for perception and the resulting understandings from this perception are the crucial experience by which entrepreneurial acting is started and gives the permission to act in the entrepreneurial functions.[7]

---

[1] Tiberius (2011), p. 13.

[2] Schneider (1995), p. 32.

[3] Freiling (2008), p. 47.

[4] Freiling (2008), p. 48.

[5] Freiling (2008), p. 48.

[6] Freiling (2008), pp. 48/49.

[7] Colwell and Narayanan (2010), p. 299.

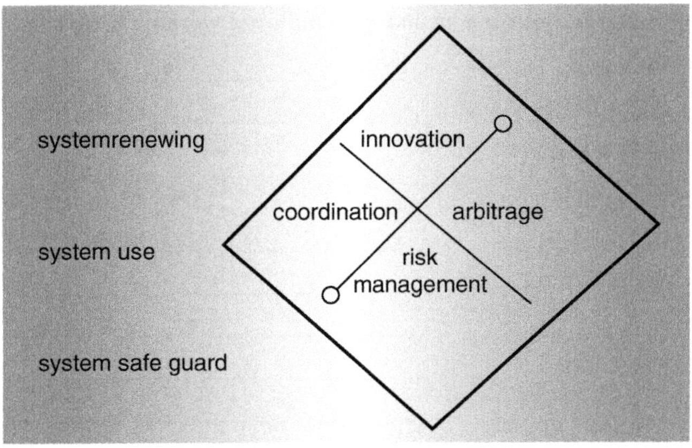

Fig. 5.1 Systematic of entrepreneurial functions (Freiling, 2005, p. 142)

This process to "see" by perception certain entrepreneurial possibilities, to combine them, and to create from these concrete actions is referred to as **entrepreneurial foresight**.

Entrepreneurial foresight is the individual, or a person, with a fixed capability for perception and the capability to bring the results of this perception under the limitations of bounded rationality along the way as action into the entrepreneurial functions.

Bounded rationality reflects on this, that an individual decider can never have all possible and impossible information. The neoclassic assumptions of reality concerning the homo oeconomicus are not appropriate.[8] The entrepreneur is limited in his borders for getting new insights. These borders are based in the individually limited capability for perception.

Perception is created by "comparing the inner incoming information of the sense with inner sensual expectations."[9] Individuals have different boarders of perception. By these different boarders of perception, they are acting in different ways by doing the entrepreneurial functions in their enterprises. The reason for individual capabilities for perception lies in the personality of the entrepreneur. "The personality of a human is understood as the whole of his personality traits: the individual differences in the physical appearance and the regularity of behavior and experience."[10] "Our reality depends on our biology."[11]

The appearance of the entrepreneur practicing the entrepreneurial functions is beside his biological and psychological constituted personality signed by his competences. Competences are cognitive abilities and skills, which can be learnt by individuals, helping them solve certain problems. Besides, competences with these cognitive abilities and skills restrict motivational, volitional, and social skills and

[8] Neumer (2012), p. 42.

[9] Eagleman (2012), p. 63.

[10] Asendorpf and Neyer (2012), p. 2.

[11] Eagleman (2012), p. 243.

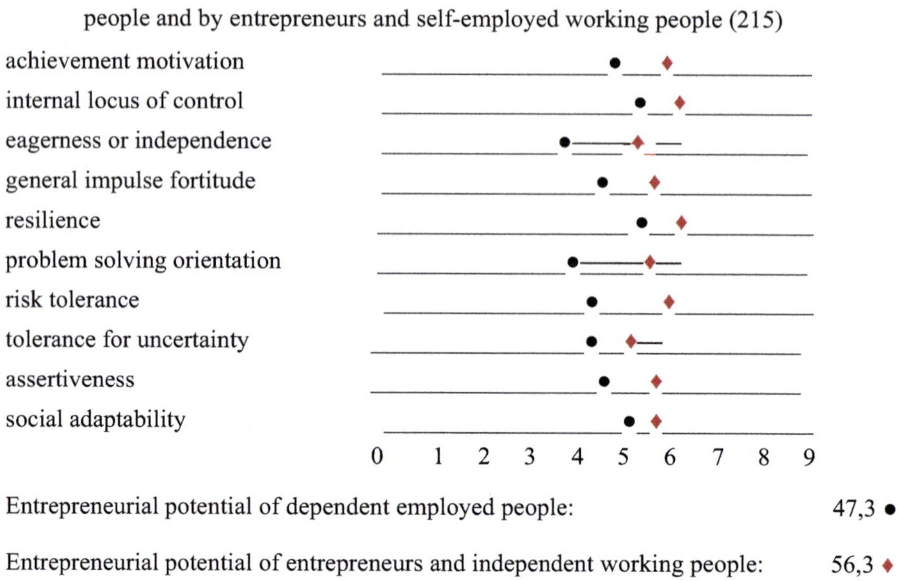

Fig. 5.2 Entrepreneurial relevant competences measured by dependent working people and by entrepreneurs and self-employed working people (215)

the willingness to use the solutions of problems in variable situations with success and responsibility.[12] Over all, the economics-accepted competences are risk tolerance, locus of control, achievement motivation, tolerance of ambiguity, eagerness for independence, assertiveness, adaptability, problem-solving orientation, emotional stability, resilience, and fortitude for impulses.[13] Regarding entrepreneurial competences, it is possible to look over the entrepreneur in economic plausible categories. Through a questionnaire technique, the following were found out (Fig. 5.2) (Müller, 2010, p.67).[14]

So, we can suppose that entrepreneurial acting people should have the following competences:

- High achievement motivation
- A very high internal locus of control
- Above average of independence
- Above average of impulse fortitude
- A very high resilience
- Average till above average problem-solving orientation
- Above average risk tolerance
- A little bit more than average tolerance for uncertainty
- A higher assertiveness
- A little bit higher than average social adaptability

[12] Weinert (2001), p. 14.

[13] Brauckmann, Bijedic, and Schneider (2008), pp. 13–17.

[14] Müller (2010), p. 67.

The criticism of this supposition is founded in the fact that the presented competences are a shortened denomination of something "in which the influences from another much more widespread social and biological system are coming in."[15] So, these are denominations for facts, which are not coming from the economics but, for example, from the psychology, the biology, the genetics, etc.

With this, from other sciences—like the psychology—facts are also important and influence economically demanded entrepreneurial competences. And these results are not developed on the ground of the economics. It is not without reason that "the psychology of the personality is anchored in those psychological processes which are the ground for the behavior and the experience of the mental healthy human, and gives answer how these processes influence themselves by building an organized system, named personality."[16] Taking psychological facts to contour the entrepreneurial personality is caused by the circumstances in which personality traits are determinants of entrepreneurial success.[17]

So, the economics of constructing "their" entrepreneurial personality are working with results from other disciplines without questioning how to explain the constructing elements of the entrepreneur as actor in the entrepreneurial functions. That means that the economics by themselves are not able to explain the personality of the entrepreneur as the main agent in the entrepreneurial functions and in the field of entrepreneurial foresight, but urgently need other academic disciplines to find results.

As mentioned before, the **person** of the entrepreneur as actor in the entrepreneurial functions comes into the focus. It is the **person**, the entrepreneur who has to perceive signals and to form signals to information. It is this person, who has to bring this information into the enterprise and who must have entrepreneurial foresight over the process of perception.

This is postulated as the central point of self-efficacy[18] and points out the demand on the person "behind" the entrepreneurial functions. So, it is necessary to learn more about the personality of the entrepreneur as a determinant of entrepreneurial acting and entrepreneurial foresight.

5.2 The Way to Interdisciplinary Bricks that Build Entrepreneurial Acting and Entrepreneurial Foresight

The individual-related fact of perception and with this the turning to the individual personality give an indication to the reciprocal relation between the filters of perception and decision. Those signals are weighted as significant, which are compatible to the preference structure of a person and with this, can pass unconsciously the personal selection filter. There is an unconscious preselection of information, which

[15] Eagleman (2012), p. 256.

[16] Rammsayer and Weber (2010), p. 17.

[17] Anger (2012), p. 4.

[18] Rammsayer and Weber (2010), p. 100.

can manifest in the action tendencies of a person.[19] So, we need to learn more about those characteristics and their construction, characterizing a person—the entrepreneur—over a longer period. It is necessary to look over those characteristics which determine in a person his/her polarization and which are seen by the person as important bricks of his/her life story (experiences, narrative).[20]

So, there is the discussion about psychological—biological processes, about cognitive processes, which create a person—the entrepreneur.[21] These processes do not only start the cognition of an object of perception, but in the same time the evaluation and the assessment of this object.[22] Perhaps, it is a question of the self-surveillance tendency that is bounded in the cognition of such an object of perception. And also, this self-surveillance tendency is meant to be the pure personal psychological ability of the entrepreneur that has entrepreneurial functions and entrepreneurial foresight. There is the question "Who does this situation want me to be and how can I be that person" in case of a high self-surveillance tendency, in contrast to the question "Who am I and how can I be me in this situation" in case of a low self-surveillance tendency.[23]

The difficult comprehensible broadness of the personality is reflected by his/her personality characteristics and his/her cognitive capabilities: "Identity and reputation shape the roles of individuals in the economy and the society to which they belong."[24]

The personality is constituted by six paradigms: (a) paradigm of characteristics, (b) paradigm of information processing, (c) the dynamic-interacting paradigm, (d) paradigm of neuroscience, (e) paradigm of molecular genetics, and (f) the evolutionary-psychological paradigm.[25] Paradigms are propositions, bundles of hypothesis or theoretical concepts.

The paradigm of characteristics tells about the individuality of a person by describing his/her characteristics. The characteristics are summarized in a personality profile.[26]

The paradigm of information processing postulates, that "human behavior and experience is grounded in the handling of information inside the nervous system, getting by receptors impulses from the environment and from the own body, which are converted into other information and are responsible for consciously experience and bring out by motor functions (activities) information to the environment."[27]

> The dynamic-interacting paradigm is understanding the development of personality as an interaction between environment and the own characteristics during the process of life.[28]

---

[19] Scheffer and Mainz (2009).

[20] Brüll (2010), pp. 21/22.

[21] Mummendey (2006), p. 25.

[22] Mummendey (2006), p. 52.

[23] Mummendey (2006), p. 62.

[24] Borghans, Goldsteyn, Heckmann, and Humphries (2011), p. 4.

[25] Asendorpf and Neyer (2012), pp. 25–78.

[26] Asendorpf and Neyer (2012), p. 26.

[27] Asendorpf and Neyer (2012), p. 33.

[28] Asendorpf and Neyer (2012), p. 39.

The paradigm of neuroscience of psychology contains a trial to explain human behavior by neuroscientific reasons.[29] This approach bases on the fact that human information processing is done by the nervous system (brain and nerves) in such a way that the smallest units of the nervous system, the neurons, serve as information carriers. So, this approach is a biological one to explain the human personality by explaining the information transfer inside the nervous system.[30]

The molecular-genetic paradigm is based on the molecular behavior genetics. This is a projection of explanation "to refer personality to the individual typical pattern of alleles."[31] "Allele" is the name for different forms of a gene.[32] "Genes are sectors on the chromosomes which are defined by their function in the metabolism. They can vary from person to person in their structure."[33] So, different alleles on the same gene are told about. The human genome was until now deciphered with about 25,000 genes. They all can appear in different patterns of alleles. As this pattern of alleles in a human is unchangeable, the conclusion is near "to refer individual particularities of the personality in individual typical patterns of alleles in the genes."[34] Today, a genetic determination of the personality is estimated by about 50%.[35] There is the supposition that different patterns of alleles are influencing the efficiency of the neurotransmitter assimilation and, with this, are influencing the biochemical information transfer. Despite this obviously serious influence of the genes on the human personality, other authors argue that not only the genes induce human behavior, but that genes and environment are working together in such a complex way that genetic determinations can bring out—depending on environment influences—overcomplex processes of brain behavior development in different ways.[36]

The evolutionary-psychological paradigm contains the demand for reasons of the fundamental existence of big differences in the personality. This is an attempt to find out differences in the personality and the personality development over the very long time in human-evolutionary processes, by which human behavior and human experience are visible.[37]

The mentioned paradigms clearly show the psychological and biological implementation of the human personality. These implementations highlight "that the numberless facets of our behavior, our thinking and our experience are depending inseparable from a very huge moist and chemical-electric network, named nervous system",[38] which by the activities of the brain rules the human action. The brain research acts on the assumption "that the personality is anchored in the brain and in

[29] Asendorpf and Neyer (2012), p. 49.
[30] Asendorpf and Neyer (2012), p. 49.
[31] Asendorpf and Neyer (2012), p. 62.
[32] Graw (2010), p. 3.
[33] Asendorpf and Neyer (2012), p. 62.
[34] Asendorpf and Neyer (2012), p. 62.
[35] Asendorpf and Neyer (2012), p. 63.
[36] Roth (2008), p. 10.
[37] Asendorpf and Neyer (2012), p. 68.
[38] Eagleman (2012), p. 8.

Emotional-cognitive characteristics	Appearance	Presumption about entrepreneurial potential
Anxiety	Not too high	Not too high anxiety, to not give too much attention
		To menacing stimuli and to have the chance
		To solve complex tasks better
Anger tendency	Middle	Not too high, but also not too low as anger tendency
		Is necessary to trigger rational problem-oriented
		Discussions about the recognition of own mistakes
Stress	Positive affectivity	Positive affectivity to avoid: Nervous behavior, depressions, frustrations, feelings of guilt, lower task tackling
Well-being	High	High subjective well-being which brings out a high self-acceptance, control about the environment, positive relationship to others, the presence of life targets, personal growth, and the ambition for autonomy
Self-esteem	High	High self-esteem with a stable self-acceptance: Necessary to recognize own weak points, to react on success and failure, to take references serious-ly, to avoid general self-doubts
Locus of control	Internal	More internal locus of control and with this adapted higher flexibility in situations and higher efficiency
Self-efficacy	High	Higher belief into self-efficacy from which depends
		Self-evaluation and promising action
Optimism	Positive	Optimistic positive main tendency, by this better cognition, stress handling, and higher efficiency.
		But no overoptimism caused by resulting misjudgment of situation

Social characteristics	Appearance	Presumption about entrepreneurial potential
Pro-social behavior	Positive	Positive pro-social behavior promotes self-confidence into the own action competences and gives a sense for justness
Empathy	High	High empathy helps to overcome economic and staff-oriented areas of conflicts and brings out coincident actions in the enterprise
Aggressivity	Middle	Middle potential of aggression, also knotted with a potential for innovation capability
Self-expression	Higher	A higher potential of self-expression is the locus for self-control, important for leadership emergence in groups and for organizational capabilities
Social support	High	High social supporting capabilities bring out the ability for creating social networks which are important for orientation possibilities in stress situations and in complex social situations

physiology, (c) needs, (d) interests, (i) attitudes, aptitudes, and (f) temperament.[49] With this, the human personality is more than only a subject of psychology but also a subject of anthropology, somatology, biology, sociology, and genetics. The personality is noticed first with the entrance into social relationships as "personality." "The personality is not preexistent but made by the exchange with the environment."[50]

In the nearer interest stands here the psychological approach, by which the (entrepreneurial) personality is contoured by personality traits. Because, this may be an approach by which the entrepreneur can be described and explained a little bit nearer, concerning his/her abilities to develop entrepreneurial foresight, to act with uncertainties that are not quantifiable.[51] With this, there are personality traits in the foreground, which means under the aspect of time and trans-situation rather stabile traits, which are grounded in the behavior and the self-evaluation of people, manifested by differences in experience and behavior.[52]

The procedure chosen here is the "Big Five Concept." This is a concept that describes the present status of literature and knowledge of the human personality best. This concept brings out, besides habitual behavioral orientations between humans, also personal differences in sectors of personal attitudes and the regions of motivation and experience.[53] "The behaviors of the person, respective of his/her reactions on particular situations, are dependent on the traits of the person, which also builds his/her behavior dispositions."[54]

The "Big Five" factor model has the following dimensions to describe the personality: neuroticism, extraversion, agreeableness, conscientiousness, and openness[55] for experience.

These are the personality traits which "in parts depend on the genetics and the brain development, in other parts are sized in the very early childhood, but are stabilized in their individual sizing very early."[56] Besides that, there are researches about correlations between the Big Five and the survival of enterprises, the working performance, and income.[57]

The contents of the Big Five can be shown together with their supposed characteristics for the entrepreneurial functions acting people like in the following:

---

[49] Rammsayer and Weber (2010), pp. 14/15.

[50] Simon (2006), pp. 10/11.

[51] Koetz (2006), p. 13.

[52] Mummendey (2006), p. 251.

[53] Gerlitz and Schupp (2005), p. 2.

[54] Brauckmann, et al. (2008), p. 6.

[55] Roth (2007), pp. 17/18.

[56] Roth (2007), p. 32.

[57] Markgraf and Löbler (2007), p. 1.

Neuroticism		
Emotional stability	Versus	Emotional lability
Stabile, calm, unhurried, content, superior, effective, bold, low emotionality		Curious, anxious, nervous, cranky, worried, sensitive, raspy, fearful, with self-pity, instable, discouraged, disheartened
Supposed for entrepreneurial acting: High emotional stability		
Extraversion		
Extraverted	Versus	Introverted
Active, convivial, communicative, optimistic, sociable, cordially, easygoing, assertive		Distant, calm, restrained, contact avoiding
Supposed for entrepreneurial acting: Higher extraverted		
Agreeableness		
Agreeable	Versus	Irreconcilable
Compassionate, kind, admiring, cordial, softhearted, warm, generous, trustful, helpful, forgiving, friendly, cooperative, sensitive		Cold, harsh, disputatious, steel-hearted, cruel, thankless, penny-pinching
Supposed for entrepreneurial acting: More less than higher agreeableness		
Conscientiousness		
Conscientious	Versus	Not conscientious
Organized, accurate, making plans ahead, effective, responsible, reliable, accurate, practical, careful, considerate		Careless, unorderly, lightheaded, irresponsible, unreliable, forgetful, chaotic, unpunctual
Supposed for entrepreneurial acting; more conscientious than not conscientious concerning innovative facts: Neutral		
Openness		
Open	Versus	Withdrawn
Broad interested, intelligent, original, imaginative, inventive, artistic, clever, eager for knowledge, intellectual, ingenious, wise		Ordinary, one-way interested, simple without depth, not intelligent
Supposed for entrepreneurial acting: High openness for experience and combined with this higher supposed probability for entrepreneurial foresight		

Finding out the Big Five underlies a lexical process: "The lexical valuation reduces step by step the whole lexicon of a language to a manageable set of trait descriptions. With this set, there can be many self-evaluations and evaluations done, with many people, by circles of acquaintances. The resulting correlative structure of similarity is packed by factor analysis to very few independent factors.[58]" But also, as the Big Five projection describes, the personality comes out of a lexical construction, let's not forget that behind the personality describing words, there are differences in the human personality to be seen, like presented above. This is due to the fact that the very strict genetic determination of the human personality must be seen. Researches about correlations between genetic influences and the Big Five show a heritability of the Big Five with about 50%, in particular, neuroticism with 48%,

[58] Asendorpf and Neyer (2012), p. 106.

extraversion with 54%, agreeableness with 45%, conscientiousness with 49%, and openness for experiences with 57%.[59] "The other 50% belong to factors of the environment. But this under the point of view that the shared environment (growing up in the same family) only has very little influence, the most important influence being the individual environment."[60]

There is some importance in taking a view on the personality that was presented before. Because: The entrepreneur must make his decisions under uncertainty. To do this, he needs beside his professional skills and a certain tolerance for risk also the structure of his personality influenced capabilities.[61] It is not to ignore that the entrepreneurial structure of personality influence entrepreneurial acting, this in matters of the from perceptions concentrated information, which reaches the entrepreneur from inside of his enterprise, but also from the markets, the politics, the environment, etc.

5.2.3 *The Self-concept and Its Importance*

Besides the shown elements of the personality like (a) the paradigms of the psychology of personality, (b) the differences in the personality, and (c) the personality traits, the discussion must be minimally completed in this article with the d) self-concept as a further cornerstone. The discussion about self-concepts is so important, because they include process-related changing results of interaction processes. With this they don't have such an outliving structure as the personality traits have.[62] The self-concept is to be understood as the "entirety of the judgments, related to a person.[63] This entirety is produced by the summary of perceptions to oneself.[64]

The general self-concept of a person is developed by the made experiences of this person, under physical, emotional, activity-related, and social aspects.[65] The subject of the self-concept is the sum of the cognitive representations, a person saves in his/her memory from him/herself.[66] The self-concept is to differ in a cognitive-evaluative component and into an affective component. The cognitive-evaluative component means a self-description of the person, the affective component contains self-evaluations—evaluated cognitions—and with this something which is named self-esteem.[67] The self-esteem of a person is the sum of her evaluated self-cognitions on the basis of made experiences in the above-mentioned sectors.

---

[59] Bouchard and McGue (2003), p. 23.

[60] Bouchard and McGue (2003), p. 23.

[61] Caliendo, Fossen, and Kritikos (2011), p. 4.

[62] Mummendey (2006), p. 15.

[63] Mummendey (2006), p. 25.

[64] Laskowski (2000), p. 15.

[65] Daig (2006), p. 29.

[66] König (2006), p. 72.

[67] König (2006), p. 72.

By this self-picture, a person is drawing for him–/herself an image that determines how the person appears with his/her action in his/her environment.[68] It depends on the self-concept of a person how they will interpret his/her received perceptions and how to act with them.[69] As defined before, entrepreneurial action in the entrepreneurial functions and to have entrepreneurial foresight, presumes perception. So, it is easy to follow from this that entrepreneurial action in the entrepreneurial functions depends on the self-concept of the acting entrepreneur. This is due to the fact that the self-concept has a selective effect on perception. Imaginations of oneself are like evidence and keeper points and with this seen like facts. Thus, it is necessary to integrate new experiences and to estimate from the perception resulting following expectations.[70]

Significant elements from the sector of self-concept, self-evaluation, and self-esteem, which are also relevant for entrepreneurial acting, can be shown in the following list in their positive and negative characteristics[71]:

Object of observation	Positive	Negative
Self-concept, self-evaluation, self-esteem (572)		
Criticism	Less accessible for criticism	More accessible for criticism
		Affinity to generalize criticism
Perception	More optimistic colored	More pessimistic colored
	Perception	Perception
Self-concept, self-evaluation, self-esteem		
Personal importance	Feels the own person minimum as important as others	Feels the own person as not so important
Own characteristics	More convinced about their own good characteristics	Less convinced about their own good characteristics
Assertiveness	Becomes more accepted with own aspects	Becomes less accepted with own aspects
New tasks	Likes more to deal with new tasks	Likes less to deal with new tasks
Future expectation	Positive, with the expectation to solve problems	Less positive with lower expectation to solve problems
Expectation for acceptance	High expectation for acceptance by the partners of interaction	Acceptance by the partners of interaction
Anxiety	Lower	Higher
Efficiency and competence for decision-making and responsibility	Is rather overestimated	Is rather underrated
Insecurity	Lower	Higher
Own targets	Rather higher	Rather lower

68 Laskowski (2000), p. 15.

69 Laskowski (2000), p. 15.

70 Laskowski (2000), pp. 22/23.

71 Laskowski (2000), pp. 32–37.

A consequence that can result by a positive ranking of the self-worth is the fact that people are more successful in difficult situations than those with a lower ranking of the self-worth. A high self-worth estimation is knotted with stability, assertiveness, affability, open-mindedness, but also with vanity, self-hubris, pride, and overdrawn self-assurance. In this context, a positive self-concept is related more to an internal than to an external locus of control.[72]

Concerning the supposition about entrepreneurial potential capacity and the bounded higher flexibility to adapt on situations and to show a higher efficiency like done with discussing the differences in the personality, this is also equivalent to the abovementioned connection between self-concept and locus of control: a positive self-concept supports the own efficiency for entrepreneurial acting.[73]

Self-concepts are to be seen as "process-related changing results of interactions and not as an entity with an outlasting structure."[74] These interaction processes are the fundamental of relevant social standard; they give the comparisons, through which people are enabled to perceive something. "In the reciprocal influence of the individual and its social environment, the individual gives to the fellow men particular impressions on oneself, and by this is functionalizing the interaction partners to form one's self-image."[75]

By this comparative process of perception, people are able to learn how occurrences are interconnected with the appearance of other occurrences, and which consequences will follow by which behavior patterns. So, people can construct a horizon of expectation about what could happen in the future. And by this, they are able to control and to regulate their behavior.[76] This statement is perhaps further evidenced that foresight-oriented entrepreneurial acting is combined with the characteristic of the self-concept that the acting person has.

There is also a connection between the Big Five personality dimensions and self-esteem: higher self-esteem correlates with lower neuroticism and higher extraversion. People with a low self-esteem are connected with a higher worth of neuroticism and a lower worth for agreeableness and conscientiousness. So, instability of self-esteem brings out a behavior with higher emotional patterns. On the other hand, people with a high self-esteem compensate fluctuation self-esteem feeling by the trial to get the environmental situation under control.[77]

The consequence for the entrepreneur is that—in the daily acting in the entrepreneurial functions as well as in a foresight-oriented process—he should have a positive self-concept to fulfill his business. As a result of this, entrepreneurs with a positive self-concept are working target oriented, caused by the fact that disturbing anxiety for failing is probably lower than having a negative self-concept.[78] "There is

[72] Laskowski (2000), p. 28.
[73] Braun, Mieg, and Neyer (2009), p. 73.
[74] Mummendey (2006), p. 15.
[75] Mummendey (2006), p. 70.
[76] Mummendey (2006), p. 15.
[77] Mummendey (2006), p. 147.
[78] Laskowski (2000), pp. 8/9.

the expectation that the ideas which people develop from themselves (self-concept) have an important impact on their henceforward self-perception and their constitution to act."[79] So, we highlight the fact that the entrepreneurial "self" must be anchored in the self-concept of the entrepreneur and that this demand for economic success is much more important than economic awareness and experiences.[80] This entrepreneurial "self" comes out, if entrepreneurial acting happens correspondent to personal ideals, and so the problems that the entrepreneur has in his enterprise are mutating into the own personal problems of the entrepreneur.[81]

5.3 Final Considerations

This research gives information about economic attended competences for the entrepreneurial functions acting person that have an interdisciplinary background. This background can explain, in part, why entrepreneurs set their actions, as they do. Entrepreneurial acting results by the process of perception from genetic, neurobiological, psychological, and sociologic components which determine the human personality: genes and the development of the brain determine about 50% of the personality, 30% are done by the very shaping age of childhood and the early youth, and the least are added in the later childhood and in the youth further socializing components which finalize the building of the personality: "Our aware personality is at every time a socialized personality which is developed during puberty and in the very early age of being grown up…."[82] This socialization happens under the influence of genetic dispositions, development of the brain, and prenatal till early childhood development and includes about 20% of the personality.[83]

Thus, a person is essentially predisposed to be able to work in the entrepreneurial functions with success correspondent to the targets of the enterprise, or not. The reality shows a picture with a modified content: The personality and the personality traits are rather stable over time, but by using entrepreneurship education, there is the assumption that personality-related characteristics of an entrepreneur can be learned (599). So, by the development of entrepreneurial action competences, the capability for entrepreneurial acting and entrepreneurial thinking can be promoted: "Core competences to be self-dependent can be gained, trained or improved by professional experience. These core competences are an important link between the lengthy, more stable personality characteristics on the one side and concrete entrepreneurial behavior on the other side."[84] Besides professional competence and competence in methods, education also improves social competences and self-competences. The

[79] Laskowski (2000), S. 9.

[80] Rövekamp (2011), pp. 338/339.

[81] Menzenbach (2012), p. 77.

[82] Roth (2007)/2013, p. 105.

[83] Roth (2007)/2013, p. 105.

[84] Müller (2013), p. 55.

advancement serves to the consolidation of affective, motivational, cognitive, and social capabilities of a person, and with this, it has an influence on the emotional stability, achievement motivation, locus of control, problem-solving orientation, tolerance of ambiguity, and assertiveness.[85] But, such a promotion doesn't change the fundamental structure which is anchored in the personality of the entrepreneur.

A direct result of how a talented entrepreneur or entrepreneurial foresight must be constructed is not to be read here. This is due to the fact that entrepreneurial foresight is only one component of entrepreneurial acting, and it also depends on the process and the ability of entrepreneurial perception. And this ability for perception is presented by the shown interdisciplinary elements. We can suppose that each entrepreneurial action also has a little bit of this entrepreneurial foresight component. Nevertheless, there are people who have by their genetic/ biological/psychological predisposition the talent to knot and to concentrate perceptions in a very special way. The results then are shown as pioneering and foresighted activities and results.

This article does not represent a closed result. The next steps are to "create" a model of an entrepreneurial personality, which beside the presented entrepreneurial competences also includes these contents, coming from the interdisciplinary field of personality research and the research of self-concept.

But also, when this step is done, a universally modeled entrepreneur will not appear as a standard to judge about the founding of new enterprises, for the capability to be a good successor in an enterprise, etc. Thus, such a universally modeled entrepreneur would not give space for different targets of the concrete enterprise. The entrepreneur with the target for profit maximizing will probably not be constructed as an entrepreneur who is directed much more in social aspects in his enterprise or as an entrepreneur who is primarily interested in the development of new marketable products.

However, related to the title of this essay, there is an answer in so far as the reader can scrutinize himself in a calm moment about the own status of his personality. Perhaps he will find out weak points that indicate he is not an entrepreneur—or he says for himself: I am highly predestined to be an entrepreneur.

References

Anger, S. (2012). Die Weitergabe von Persönlichkeitseigenschaften und intellektuellen Fähigkeiten von Eltern an ihre Kinder. *DIW Wochenbericht.*, ISSN0012-1304, *79*(29), 3–12.

Asendorpf, J. B., & Neyer, F. J. (2012). In J. B. Asendorpf & F. J. Neyer (Eds.), *Psychologie der Persönlichkeit* (p. 5). Berlin, Germany: Springer. Auflage.

Bijedic, T. (2013). 'Unternehmerisch handeln macht Schule' Legitimation, Voraussetzun-gen und Ergebnisse einer Entrepre-neurship Education in der Sekundarstufe II. *Zeitschrift für ökonomische Bildung (ZföB), 01*, 44–72.

Borghans, L., Goldsteyn, B., Heckmann, J., & Humphries, J. (2011). Identification problems in personality psychologiy. *Schriftenreihe METEOR/Maastricht Research School of Economics of Technology and Organizations, 11*, 25.

[85] Bijedic (2013), p. 57.

Bouchard, T., & McGue, M. (2003). Genetic and environmental influences on human psychological differences. *Journal of Neurobiology, 54*, 4–45.
Brauckmann, U., Bijedic, T., & Schneider, D. (2008). *Unternehmerische Persönlichkeit - eine theoretische Rekonstruktion und normaldefinitorische Konturierung, Schumpeter school of business and economics*. Wuppertal, Germany: Bergische Universität Wuppertal.
Braun, A., Mieg, H., & Neyer, F. J. (2009). Sind Erfinder anders als es die psychologische Forschung erwarten lässt? *Wirtschaftspsychologie, 1*, 69–79.
Brüll, M. (2010). *Akademisches Selbstkonzept und Bezugsgruppenwechsel*. Göttingen, Germany: Hogrefe Verlag.
Caliendo, M., Fossen, F. M., & Kritikos, A. (2011). *Personality characteristics and the decision to become and stay self-employed*. Berlin, Germany: Deutsches Institut für Wirtschaftsforschung. 2011, ECONIS-Online. Katalog der ZBW.
Colwell, K., & Narayanan, V. K. (2010). Foresight in economic development policy: Shaping the institutional vontext for entrepreneurial innovation. *Futures, 45*(2010), 295–303.
Daig, I. (2006). *Male gender role dysfunction*. Dissertation, FB Erziehungs-wissenschaften und Psychologie, FU Berlin.
Eagleman, D. (2012). *Inkognito, die geheimen Eigenleben unseres Gehirns*. Frankfurt am Main, Germany: Campus Verlag GmbH.
Freiling, J. (2005). Unternehmerfunktionen als Brücke zwischen Marketing und Innovationsmanagement. In J. Freiling (Ed.), *Technologiemanagement & Marketing – Herausforderungen eines integrierten Innovati-onsmanagements* (pp. 133–154). Wiesbaden, Germany: Deutscher Universitäts-verlag.
Freiling, J. (2008). Unternehmerfunktionen und Gründungsmanagement. In J. Freiling (Ed.), *Entrepreneurship. Theorien und Fallstudien zu Gründungs- Wachstums- und KMU Management*. Wien, Austria: Facultas Verlags- und Buchhandels, AG.
Gerlitz, J.-Y., & Schupp, J. (2005). Zur Erhebung der Big-Five-basierten Persönlich-keitsmerkmale im SOEP. In *Dokumentation der Instrumentenentwicklung BFI-S auf Basis des SOEP-Pretests 2005*. Berlin, Germany: DIW Berlin (Deutsches Institut für Wirtschaftsforschung).
Graw, J. (2010). *Genetik* (5th ed.). Berlin, Germany: Springer.
Koetz, E. (2006). *Persönlichkeitsstile und unternehmerischer Erfolg von Existenzgründern*. Dissertation Lehreinheit Psychologie: Universität Osnabrück im Fachbereich Humanwissenschaften.
König, J. (2006). *Sekundarschulen als differenzielle Entwicklungsmilieus?* Dissertation, FB Erziehungswissenschaft und Psychologie, FU Berlin.
Laskowski, A. (2000). *Was den Menschen antreibt. Entstehung und Beeinflussung des Selbstkonzepts*. Frankfurt, Germany: Campus-Verlag.
Markgraf, D., & Löbler, H. (2007). *Persönlichkeit und wirtschaftliche Orientierung als Einflussgrößen auf den Unternehmensgründungsprozess*. Leipzig, Germany: Universität Leipzig – Lehrstuhl für BWL insb. Marketing – Veröffentlichungen.
Menzenbach, J. (2012). *Visionäre Unternehmensführung*. Fachmedien, Wiesbaden: Springer-Gabler, Springer.
Müller, G. F. (2010). Unternehmerische Eignung – Impuls – und Erfolgsfaktoren für eine erfolgreiche berufliche Selbständigkeit. In *Psychologische Expertise für erfolgreiches Unternehmertum in Deutschland*.Berufsverband Deutscher Psychologinnen und Psychologen e.V. (Hrsg.). Berlin, Germany: Deutscher Psychologen Verlag.
Müller, Günter F. (2013). *Berufliche Selbständigkeit*. In: Wirtschaftspsychologie, K. Moser (Hrsg.), Springer, Berlin, Germany, 379–398.
Mummendey, H. D. (2006). *Psychologie des Selbst*. Göttingen, Germany: Hogrefe Verlag.
Neumer, J. (2012). Entscheiden unter Ungewissheit. Von der bounded rationality zum situativen Handeln. In: Fritz Böhle, Sigird Busch (Hrsg.): Management von Ungewissheit. Transcript Verlag.
Rammsayer, T., & Weber, H. (2010). *Differentielle Psychologie - Persönlich-keitstheorien*. Göttingen, Germany: Hogrefe Verlag.
Roth, G. (2003). *Fühlen, denken, handeln. Wie das Gehirn unser Verhalten steuert*. Frankfurt, Germany: Suhrkamp Verlag.

Roth, G. (2007). *Persönlichkeit, Entscheidung und Verhalten* (8th ed.). Klett-Cotta. Auflage 2013.

Roth, G. (2008). Hirnforschung. Homo neuro-biologicus- ein neues Menschenbild? *Aus Politik und Zeitgeschichte*, 44–45, 2008.

Rövekamp, Cornelia. (2011). *Was unterscheidet erfolgreiche von weniger erfolgreichen Gründerinnen?: Qualitaitve Längsschnittuntersuchung von Kleinstunternehmer/–innen*. Dissertation, Freie Universität Berlin.

Rudolph, U. (2007). Soziales Verhalten. In: Stemmler, G. (Hrsg.) Enzyklopädie der Emotionen. Göttingen, Germany: Hogrefe, 2007.Kapitel 11.

Scheffer, D., & Mainz, D. (2009). *Messung von impliziten Persönlichkeits-Systemen mit Hilfe der visuellen Testmethode des Visual Questionnaire ViQ: Arbeitspapiere der Nordakademie*. Elmshorn, Germany: Hochschule der Wirtschaft.

Schneider, D. (1995). *Betriebswirtschaftslehre Band 1: Grundlagen*. München, Germany: Oldenbourg Verlag.

Simon, W. (Hrsg.). (2006). Persönlichkeitsmodelle und Persönlichkeitstests. GABAL Verlag GmbH, Offenbach, Germany.

Tiberius, V. (Hrsg.). (2011). Zukunftsorientierung in der Betriebswirtschaftslehre. Gabler Verlag, Wiesbaden, Germany.

Weber, H., & Rammsayer, T. (Hrsg.). (2005). Handbuch der Persönlichkeitspsy-chologie und Differentiellen Psychologie. Hofgrefe Verlag, Göttingen, Germany.

Weinert, F. E. (2001). Vergleichende Leistungsmessung in Schulen - eine umstrittene Selbstverständlichkeit. Zitiert bei: Kompetenzentwicklung und Wissensmanagement im Kontext des lebenslangen Lernens und ihre Thematisierung in der Öffentlichkeit, Katharina M. Baumeister, Inauguraldissertation, Ludwig-Maximilians-Universität München, Fakultät für Psychologie und Pädagogik, 2009 Department Psychologie, Organisations- und Wirtschafts-psychologie.

Chapter 6
Scientific Selling: Improving Sales Performance Through Applied Psychology. Case Study on a Romanian Company

Mihai Talpoş and Denis Dan

Abstract The incompatibilities that frequently emerge between certain products or services and a series of particular segments of potential clients are due, in a higher degree that we could imagine, to some psychocultural fundaments incorrectly conducted or understood by organizations that promote those products or services in the market.

For any sales professionals, it should be hard to design a daring sales objective on a certain segment of potential clients without basing ideas on a minimal understanding of the psychological or psychocultural profile of the targeted clients. If the sales actions initiated by a certain company do not complement the psychological characteristics of the targeted client segment, the chances that the products or services promoted to be rejected increase dramatically.

Unfortunately, there are still insufficient companies that understand the fact that the current sales management should be analyzed and understood not only from a unidirectional (mono-disciplinary) perspective but also from a complex perspective, relevant both from a scientific point of view and also from a social, economic, or even psychological one.

In such a context, the present paper aims to be of help both for sales managers or practitioners and also for theoreticians, with a perspective on the sales act, in general, approached from a multi-, inter-, plural-, and even transdisciplinary point of view, at the congruence between multiple disciplines, such as sales management, communication, fashion psychology, process communication, neurolinguistics programming, social psychology, cultural psychology, or psycholinguistics.

The work even suggests a comprehensive working tool: personality inventory of the shoppers, which may have concrete uses in the sales domain.

M. Talpoş (✉) • D. Dan
Emanuel University of Oradea, Oradea, Romania
e-mail: mihai.talpos@emanuel.ro; denis94dan@gmail.com

S. Văduva et al. (eds.), *Solutions for Business, Culture and Religion in Eastern Europe and Beyond*, DOI 10.1007/978-3-319-63369-5_6

Keywords Sales • Practical psychology • Process communication • Personality types

6.1 Introduction

Habits (including the ones connected to clothing and "looks") are fed by people in many ways and with many efforts.[1] People, in general, organize their environment in a manner that describes them; they choose a certain type of clothing and looks (which they consider representative for them) and have the tendency to keep their choices for as long as possible. If we add on to this tendency the fact that other people from the communities they live in expect them to act predictably, the repetitiveness of habits, including the clothing ones, manifested by those people, is consolidated.[2]

The clients, as all people, live based on a series of norms established by themselves, and they set their own values and beliefs.[3] These become, in time, true action principles, which we can find in the behavior of clients, including in their buying behavior.

Even when it comes to clothing, a clothing habit can be translated in a certain type of behavior. A person with tasteful and tidy clothing is most of the times a person that has already formed concrete convictions regarding their own person. If these beliefs state that the respective person is a pleasant one, the beliefs will be strengthened through behavior. The person will be capable of getting close to people much easier and with more openness and will be more sociable, prompting feelings of pleasantness in people around him or her.[4]

This research paper aims to contribute to the effort of offering a pertinent answer to the question related to the degree in which a person's predictable behavior can manifest certain traits of clothing personality and can help sales practitioners appeal to a more efficient, much better psychologically anchored sales discourse on which clients build their buying decision. Clothing habits, as any habits, are supported and maintained by a series of resorts identified in neurolinguistics programming (NLP) shaped as an anchor. The anchors are transforming stimuli for the human behavior, which launch in people internal mechanisms that determine them to react in a certain way.[5] The visual anchors offered by clothing can function as real triggers for certain types of reactions or emotional states.[6] If we add words to these visual anchors, which, as process communication theories teach us, can also

[1] O'Connor and Lages (2009), p. 22.

[2] Ibid, pp. 160–161.

[3] Ibid.

[4] Ibid.

[5] Ibid, p. 192.

[6] Ibid.

be efficient anchors, the personality of the analyzed subject starts to be deciphered, so that the assumptions that can be made regarding the behavior of the respective person can become more correct. Nevertheless, since the 1980s, Rodger Bailey[7] demonstrated that people that use certain words in specific situations have predictable behaviors.[8]

Identifying, in order to satisfy the needs of the clients that a sales practitioner interacts with, requires, in many cases, giving or receiving recognition signs.[9] This is done with difficulty because the majority of sales practitioners, due to lack of "collateral" training, in niched domains such as psychology practice in general, clothing psychology in particular, and other sciences such as NLP, process communication or even advertisement psychology. It is important, therefore, that these sales agents acquire the capacity of observing, analyzing, and understanding clients' traits and behavior, so they can knowingly react in their effort to obtain the so-called permissions granted by clients in sales communication.

The absence of recognition signs related to verbal or behavioral communication leads sales agents, detail-oriented people, in an area of informational penury regarding the respective clients that manifest such an attitude. A good chance of overcoming a deadlock such as this one is their adaptability to deal with the situation and resorting to practices of recognition of client's psychological profile, practices that are related to the visual side of interaction, or—in other words—practices that are related to the personality of the clothing and the exterior aspect.

Once recognized and capitalized, the relevant signs that help categorize clients in certain personality typologies and implicitly in certain behavioral bands can generate apparently spontaneous changes in the attitude of shoppers. In the majority of cases though, it is not enough for sales agents to learn to correctly categorize clients in different types of personality and properly communicate with them but also correlate signs and answers received from clients with certain specific characteristics of the products and services they are selling, so that their approach truly brings added efficiency in sales.

The analysis of psychological attributes that is made purely at a clothing level can therefore be insufficient. Not coincidentally, classic works developed until now in regard to psychological profiling based on clothing criteria have been accompanied by a certain doubtfulness regarding their scientific value. Regardless, as demonstrated before, on the background of extending preoccupations of multi-, pluri-, and even transdisciplinary level, sales management can gain the force and scientific maturity needed to relevantly approaching this theme.

---

[7] Researcher and psycholinguist Rodger Bailey is the creator of the *L.A.B. Profile—Language and Behavior Profile* system, able to extract relevant information from people's language and behavior.

[8] Santangelo (2011).

[9] Collingnon (2015), p. 86.

6.2 Research Methodology

The research methodology process at the basis of the present paper is the one presented in Fig. 6.1 and can be placed in the category of classic scientific research approaches.

As stated before, *the interest area* of the paper is in fact the congruency area of multiple disciplines, such as sales management, practical psychology, clothing psychology, advertisement psychology, process communication, or even neurolinguistics programming.

The main hypothesis that was used to start the scientific research presented here is the one that by systematically analyzing certain clothing and personality looks and traits that clients have, with the help of a scientific instrument, especially developed to serve this purpose—the personality inventory based on clothing psychology—sales practitioners can increase their efficiency considerably.

The bibliographic study that was mentioned while the research was undertaken was an intense and varied one, with no less than 40 bibliographic landmarks consulted, in an effort that targeted the following operational objectives: clarifying, defining, or explaining the terms, notions, and concepts specific to the domains included in the interest area and used in the work; respecting a modern scientific language with a dynamic evolution; the possibility of offering examples and concrete references, as precise and without fault as possible; and presenting solutions and avant-gardist ideas in a credible way. Therefore, information sources of the most diverse spectrum, such as specialized books and articles, online articles, websites, online audio-video materials, press articles, and even press releases, were used.

The work methodology required eight interdependent steps, the research team understanding the fact that ensuring the methodologic coherence represents the key of the experiment included in the phase of collecting and analyzing data. The eight stages were:

1. Identifying the main types of clothing personality and the levels of manifestation of the most important aspects that characterize each personality type (clothes, accessories, colors, hairstyle).
2. Determining the correspondence between clothing personality types and personality types identified in the process communication theory and spotting the main behaviors which can be associated to each personality type.

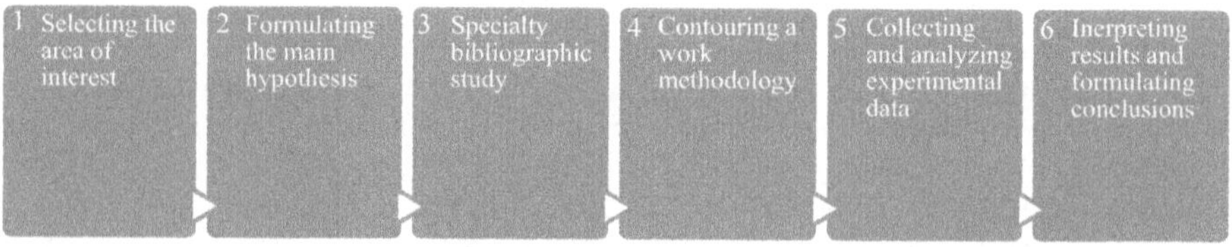

Fig. 6.1 Research process. Source: Popa

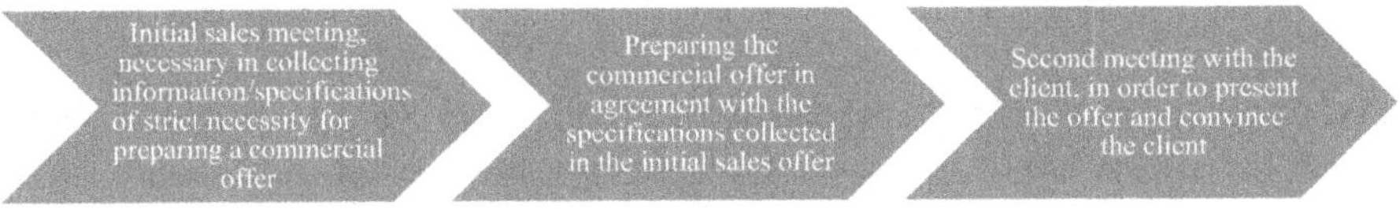

Fig. 6.2 Work model (on a sales line)

3. Designing an observation grid of the aspects that characterize each type of clothing personality.
4. Applying the work tool (observation grid) through an experimental program hold within a limited liability company which has as work model (on a sales line) presented in Fig. 6.2.
5. The analysis of the data collected in the first sales meeting, interpretation of the results of the experiment, and determining the presumptive clothing psychological profile of each client included in the experimental program.
6. Preparing the offer and the speech that was needed to be applied by sales agents in the second sales meeting they were about to have with each client included in the experimental program, in relation to the buying behavior they could manifest, in agreement to the psychological clothing profile they were categorized in.
7. Evaluating the impact that the use of practical psychology tools in sales had on the sales the company had.
8. Issuing suggestions regarding the improvement of the tools used and identifying possible future directions of development.

Identifying the main clothing personality types was made in reference to the specialized literature consulted in the documentation stage of the research, this literature (Vilaruel, 2010) defining six large types of clothing personality: classic, trendy, dramatic, romantic, creative, and bohemian. Referring to the characteristics of the personality types identified in the process creation theory, Gerard Collingnon mentions in 2015, empathetic, thinker, rebel, perseverant, promotor, and imaginative, the research went on to determine the existing correspondence between the types of clothing personality and types of personality within process communication, as a starting point in determining the possible buying behaviors the clients analyzed from this perspective of practical psychology may have in a concrete business/acquisition context. The way in which this correspondence between the two psychological personality types was done and also the buying behaviors associated to each typology in particular are the ones presented in Table 6.1.

The collection of the experimental data was done over a period of 4 months (2016), and the experimental program was going to be conducted within the Maridan Instalcom, LLC in Ineu town, Arad County, Romania. The experimental

Table 6.1 Buying behaviors

Personality type	Behavior	Explanations regarding the behavior associated to the personality type
Classic	Rational	Base their decisions on logical thinking and are well informed when making a purchase
Trendy	Insistent	Express persuasion and are determined to obtain all they want when making a purchase, having negotiation skills, without expressing their needs
Dramatic	Difficult	Characterized as sophisticated and hard to convince people. They prefer to receive information fast because they make up their minds fast in the buying process
Romantic	Sociable	Are a communicative type, state their needs when buying something, and they let the sales agent lead them throughout the process
Creative	Spontaneous	Energetic people that make up their minds on the spot about buying or not, depending on how their attention is captured
Bohemian	Decent	Have a calm behavior, without many requirements, and do not express their personal needs

Collingnon (2015), pp. 91–93

program will consist in 30 experiments independent of the initial relationship with the same number of mentioned societies. The units in the referenced population (clients) will be easily identified due to the fact that they interacted with Maridan Instalcom, LLC. Basically, there will not be any criterion used to select the units from the reference population (the clients), because taking into consideration the reduced volume, the exhaustive investigation of the entire population was found to be opportune.

The objectives of the experimental program will be:

1. Applying the scale for data collection regarding the possible psychological profile based on clothing and look aspects by surveying the population, represented by the total of clients which Maridan Instalcom, LLC will interact with in the reference period. The validation of the quality of choices made regarding the main aspects that characterize the types of personality identified by clothing psychology
2. Validation of the personality inventory based on clothing psychology as a useful tool for sales
3. Refining and processing data collected by applying the tool to all clients with which the mentioned LLC will interact
4. Identifying the main obstacles in implementing and using on a large scale the mentioned tool but also the possible ways of improving the instrument

The investigation method used will be the direct observation, made by three independent observers, present at the interactions which the sales representative

Table 6.2 Checklist of data collection for the results of the observations

Analyzed aspects	Possible characteristics	Please check the characteristics you encounter	Succinct explanations regarding the characteristics observed (where needed)
Clothes	Comfortable		
	High quality		
	Original, creative		
	Classic		
	Structured		
	Practical		
Accessories	Hat/fur cap/cap		
	Earrings		
	Shawl/scarf/necklace		
	Watch/bracelets/rings		
	Belt/bag		
	Shoes		
Colors	Blue		
	Red		
	Yellow		
	Black		
	White		
	Green		
Hairstyle	Very neat (almost perfect)		
	Trendy style		
	Thrown back		
	Natural, easy to style		
	"Military" style (short cuts)		
	Negligent, undone		

of the LLC will have with the clients. In order to ensure a high quality of the investigation endeavor, the observers will benefit from a complete training regarding the used methodology, offered by the research team. The observation made within each independent experiment which will take place with the referenced units from the reference population (the clients) will be done with the help of a special checklist made by the research team for this particular experimental program (see Table 6.2).

The checklist comprised four main columns associated to the most important aspects which characterized each type of clothing and look (clothes, accessories, colors, hairstyle) personality. For the four columns, the possible options on the checklist to be marked by the person observing will be the ones presented in

Table 6.2 and will be in correlation to the possible forms of manifestation of the clothing and look personality identified by the research team in the specialized literature. The checklist will be preset on five people, in order to check the accessibility degree but also to avoid the ambiguity of certain phrasing and to estimate the time needed to complete it.

A number of three observers will be used, so as to attenuate as much as possible the subjective character of the observation process. This way, at the end of each interaction between the sales agents and clients, the latter ones will be analyzed based on a number of three different grids, filled by the three independent observers.

After the data is collected, the research team processed the information, associating each aspect analyzed by the observers to a type of psychological profile manifested for the majority of time, determined in correlation to the nature of the observations marked by the observers in the grids. In this way the information systematized in the Table 6.3 was used in a fast manner.

In this way, a centralizer of the possible personality types based on the results marked in the checklist by each observer was created, for each client (see Table 6.4).

The final classification of each unit from the reference population (clients) in one of the clothing personality types that were identified was made using one, two, or three of the following criteria:

1. The frequency of appearance of the clothing personality typology suggested by the aspects identified by the observers, on each of the analyzed subjects
2. The gender of the subjects (feminine or masculine), knowing the fact that specialized literature sets a series of predispositions toward certain types of personality, according to the gender
3. The detailed interpretation of the supplementary explanations offered by observers (in case the first two classification criteria did not bring conclusive results)

Therefore, at the end of the experimenting program, the following will be found:

- The number of clients that could be split in the classic, trendy, dramatic, romantic, creative, and bohemian personality type out of a total of 30 clients the company will interact (in sales) in the reference period
- The percentage of sales increase in the reference period following adapting the sales pitch and the offers to the behavior characteristics found for each client included in the experimental program, versus the same period of the previous year

Table 6.3 Criteria to determine the clothing personality type. Source: Vilaruel (2010)

Personality type	Aspects analyzed	Possible characteristics	Explanations regarding the most likely forms of appearance
Classic	Clothes	Comfortable	These people wear – usually – conservativ clothing (classic) characterized by straight lines and simplicity
		High quality	
		Original, creative	
		Classic	
		Structured	
		Practical	
	Accessories	Hat/fur cap/cap	The classical personality tends to use delicate accessories, classic watches and jewelry, that do not stand out. When a person of this personality wears a bag, it will most likely match the shoes
		Earrings	
		Shawl/scarf/necklace	
		Watch/bracelets/rings	
		Belt/bag	
		Shoes	
	Colors	Blue	The classic personality is inclined to use neutral colors, such as black or blue
		Red	
		Yellow	
		Black	
		White	
		Green	
	Hairstyle	Very neat (almost perfect	When it comes to hairstyle, classic personalities have a minimalist style, elegant and well kept
		Trendy style	
		Thrown back	
		Natural, easy to style	
		"Military" style (short cuts)	
		Negligent, undone	
Trendy	Clothes	Comfortable	The clothing of people manifesting the characteristics of the trendy personality is original, lacking the constraints of traditional fashion and tends to find its support especially in the casual-sporty area
		High quality	
		Original, creative	
		Classic	
		Structured	
		Practical	
	Accessories	Hat/fur cap/cap	The trendy personality tends to use shiny accessories: large earrings, golden necklaces, or anything that will draw attention and is fashionable
		Earrings	
		Shawl/scarf/necklace	
		Watch/bracelets/rings	
		Belt/bag	
		Shoes	
	Colors	Blue	Trendy people prefer bold colors, that have red as a basis (eclectic pink) and electric blue
		Red	
		Yellow	
		Black	
		White	
		Green	

(continued)

Table 6.3 (continued)

	Hairstyle	Very neat (almost perfect Trendy style Thrown back Natural, easy to style "Military" style (short cuts) Negligent, undone	The hairstyle of trendy people may vary between styles, but all these styles have a common denominator: they're in fashion
Dramatic	Clothes	Comfortable High quality Original, creative Classic Structured Practical	The people with this kind of personality prefer sophisticated, glittery, shiny, sensual clothes (tight) that would transmit visible hints regarding their social status
	Accessories	Hat/fur cap/cap Earrings Shawl/scarf/necklace Watch/bracelets/rings Belt/bag Shoes	Dramatic people's accessories are true declarations of power. They prefer expensive watches, shoes, belts and bags of high quality (most times leather) and products from well-known brands
	Colors	Blue Red Yellow Black White Green	Dramatic people use high-contrast colors (black/white; red/black; green/red) combining them with boldness [11]
	Hairstyle	Very neat (almost perfect Trendy style Thrown back Natural, easy to style "Military" style (short cuts) Negligent, undone	The hairstyle dramatic persons usually have is a mix of classic and trendy, most times the choices made in this category are destined to accentuate the features of the face, prominent cheekbones, angular lips, or prominent nose
Romantic	Clothes	Comfortable High quality Original, creative Classic Structured Practical	When it comes to clothes, romantic people prefer clothes with little details (lace, frills), all marked by good taste and beauty
	Accessories	Hat/fur cap/cap Earrings Shawl/scarf/necklace Watch/bracelets/rings Belt/bag Shoes	The accessories they prefer are delicate jewelry (many times passed on from one generation to the other), but also hats able to draw moderate attention from the audience, due to their charm

(continued)

Table 6.3 (continued)

	Colors	Blue	The colors they prefer are mainly delicate (white, yellow or light green) but dark colors are not excluded (burgundy red, black) as long as they're used in moderation
		Red	
		Yellow	
		Black	
		White	
		Green	
	Hairstyle	Very neat (almost perfect	The romantic category adds a touch of seduction and sensuality, betting on the effect of natural curls, able to highlight the delicate cheekbones (most times) and friendly face
		Trendy style	
		Thrown back	
		Natural, easy to style	
		"Military" style (short cuts)	
		Negligent, undone	
Creative	Clothes	Comfortable	The clothing creative people have is unconventional (unusual prints), daring and with the influence of multiple styles (most times from the trendy and romantic sphere)
		High quality	
		Original, creative	
		Classic	
		Structured	
		Practical	
	Accessories	Hat/fur cap/cap	Creative people call for accessories, indicating they do not care about other people's opinion: uncommon hats, extravagant shawls, or unconventional shoes
		Earrings	
		Shawl/scarf/necklace	
		Watch/bracelets/rings	
		Belt/bag	
		Shoes	
	Colors	Blue	The creative persons prefer high-impact color combinations (electric blue or daring pink), which highlight their personality and self-confidence
		Red	
		Yellow	
		Black	
		White	
		Green	
	Hairstyle	Very neat (almost perfect	Their hairstyle combines more styles in one, because at this chapter they orient themselves after what they think they like and suits them best
		Trendy style	
		Thrown back	
		Natural, easy to style	
		"Military" style (short cuts)	
		Negligent, undone	

(continued)

Table 6.3 (continued)

Bohemian	Clothes	Comfortable	Their clothing is comfortable as a concept and auto-expressive, most times marked by retro prints, unconventional or even with an ethnical character
		High quality	
		Original, creative	
		Classic	
		Structured	
		Practical	
	Accessories	Hat/fur cap/cap	Tied to the clothing options, the accessories bohemians prefer are hats with jewelry applied on them, Indian bracelets, hippy hairbands, or, in general, "flower power" accessories
		Earrings	
		Shawl/scarf/necklace	
		Watch/bracelets/rings	
		Belt/bag	
		Shoes	
	Colors	Blue	Bohemians prefer rich yet neutral colors (brown), but also the ones that have a connection to life (green, blue, red)
		Red	
		Yellow	
		Black	
		White	
		Green	
	Hairstyle	Very neat (almost perfect	Bohemians' hairstyle can be labeled as eccentric, with hippy inclinations and without too much attention given to a neat appearance of the hair
		Trendy style	
		Thrown back	
		Natural, easy to style	
		"Military" style (short cuts)	
		Negligent, undone	

Table 6.4 The frequency of reoccurrence of the aspect that suggests a certain personality type

Client 1						
Observer's number	Frequency of appearance of the aspects that suggest a certain type of personality					
	Classic	Trendy	Dramatic	Romantic	Creative	Bohemian
1	1	1	0	2	0	0
2	2	1	0	0	0	0
3	0	0	0	4	0	0
Total	3	2	0	6	0	0

6.3 Conclusion

The initiative of studying an extremely complex domain—client/consumer behavior—goes very well with the current trends in science which promote the study of complex phenomena through multi-, inter-, plural-, and transdisciplinary approaches.

Table 6.5 Percentage reference regarding peoples' gender

Reference percentage of the type of persons analyzed		
Personality type	Men (%)	Women (%)
Empathic	16	44
Thinker	38	12
Rebel	16	24
Perseverant	15	5
Promotor	7	3
Imaginative	8	12

The paper does not stop at simply listing/analyzing aspects that have to do with clothing psychology, because those aspects considered relevant are included in a comprehensive work tool that can have concrete uses in sales area. The work creates therefore a theoretical-methodological framework useful to sales practitioners (particularly) and entrepreneurs (in general).

If the analysis levels are modified/extended, more differentiating attributes between personality types can be found, and on their background a tool can be built that will capitalize in sales the specific/significant differences that emerge in clients' personality typologies.

Following the study on personality types from the process communications, certain percentage differences were found regarding the gender of the analyzed people, presented in Table 6.5.

The study of this paper requires a similar evaluation with this analysis model, due to the fact that it presents the characteristics and percentage references of the clothing personality types that were identified.

6.4 Research/Paper Limitations

- The discrepancy between "how we dress" and "how we are" or "how we behave."
- Psychological profiling is a multilevel analysis endeavor, but the present paper has wanted to approach only the analysis made from the clothing psychology level.
- Each person presents characteristics of multiple personality types (although there is a dominant one), and interpretation errors can occur.

6.5 Directions of Possible Development

- Clothing personality on Facebook
- Extending the endeavor of visualization of a model of psychological categorization/profiling of the shopper from a wider perspective, at least from the point of view of the psychological specialization (i.e., social psychology, cultural psychology, psycholinguistic psychology, etc.).

Appendix

Personality type	Aspects analyzed	Degree of importance in determining the clothing personality type				
		Very high	High	Medium	Low	Very low
Classic	Clothes					
	Accessories					
	Colors					
	Hairstyle					
Trendy	Clothes					
	Accessories					
	Colors					
	Hairstyle					
Dramatic	Clothes					
	Accessories					
	Colors					
	Hairstyle					
Romantic	Clothes					
	Accessories					
	Colors					
	Hairstyle					
Creative	Clothes					
	Accessories					
	Colors					
	Hairstyle					
Bohemian	Clothes					
	Accessories					
	Colors					
	Hairstyle					

References

Collingnon, G. (2015). *Cum sa le spun … Process communication*. Bucharest, Romania: Trei Publishing House.

O'Connor, J., & Lages, A. (2009). *Coaching cu NLP*. Bucharest, Romania: Curtea veche.

Popa, L. *Aspecte generale privind cercetarea stiintifica.* Internet Article. Retrieved April 27, 2016, from http://sorana.academicdirect.ro/pages/doc/Doc2012/_materiale/MCS_Curs.pdf

Santangelo, J. (2011). *What is the LAB profile?* Internet Article. Retrieved March 24, 2016, from http://www.prosoftskills.com/Pages/WhatisNLP.aspx

Vilaruel, A. (2010). You have a classic clothing personality. *The Chic Fashionista.* Retrieved April 4, 2016, from http://www.thechicfashionista.com/classic-clothing-personality.html#Top

Internet Resources

http://www.forbes.com/sites/learnvest/2012/04/03/what-your-clothes-say-about-you/#6d8a960e413d.

Chapter 7
The Need for Mentoring in the Preuniversity Educational System

Curta Iosif Viorel

Abstract Mentoring novice teachers, young people who need guidance and help to adjust to the new culture is more than a necessity. Most novice teachers have never experienced the benefits of a mentoring program. Schools should be different, welcoming, and very open to provide support to young teachers. Initiation includes all activities that novice teachers are trained and supported to meet the mission and philosophy of the school, in such a way that they are part of a team. The mentoring process is difficult but necessary for beginners. In the school context, a mentor is an experienced teacher involved in supporting a novice teacher within the school. As schools become true acculturation areas where young teachers would feel welcome, accepted, and supported until they are able to master both the class of students and the contents taught, there is a need for a mentoring program according to the specific nature of each school. Each school is unique, so it is important that trainee teachers should be helped to deal with the troublesome cultural context of the new school community.

Keywords Mentor • Mentoring • School community • Initiation • Experience

7.1 Introduction

What expectations can a young teacher in his first year in the educational system have in a school where he does not know anyone and has to teach a subject he is theoretically prepared for with just a few pedagogic practical classes? His expectations are clearly high; he would like to benefit from his new colleagues' support or his schoolmasters' support in order to help him figure out the troublesome labyrinth of the unknown system he has just entered.

The path to becoming a good teacher is full of obstacles that can hinder or discourage a beginner or can dishearten a teacher so seriously that some of them give

C.I. Viorel (✉)
Liceul Teologic Baptist "Emanuel", Bd. Decebal nr. 45, Oradea, Romania
e-mail: iosifcurta@yahoo.com

S. Văduva et al. (eds.), *Solutions for Business, Culture and Religion in Eastern Europe and Beyond*, DOI 10.1007/978-3-319-63369-5_7

up after their first year. Ideally, a candidate for teaching will receive complex and rigorous academic studies as content, thorough pedagogic, methodological, and assessment preparation, having teaching opportunities even before obtaining his bachelor or master degree. After 1 or 2 years in which the teacher enters a "comprehensive induction" program (Drexler 2011), he will be able to attain his goals. This implies that the beginner still needs support, guidance, preparation, and supervision as well as many opportunities to grow professionally.

7.2 What Is a Mentor?

The term *mentor* has its origin in Homer's *Odyssey*. When Odysseus, Ithaca's king, leaves for battle in the Trojan War, he also leaves his house, his wife, and his son, Telemachus, in the care of Mentor, who was serving as a teacher and supervisor for Telemachus. After the war, Telemachus, accompanied by Mentor, goes to seek for his father, overcoming many obstacles with the help of Mentor's good training, thus showing the process efficiency. In time, the word "mentor" has become a synonym for a reliable *friend*, *advisor*, *teacher*, *guide*, and *wise person*.

The term "*mentor*" is nowadays becoming more and more popular, although it has a different meaning for different people, in different activity areas. Mentoring is just one of the ways in which one can support a person; it can be a very efficient way of bringing much satisfaction in the preparation process.

From a socio-human perspective, the *mentor* is that person who encourages, advises, and offers support to another person in order to help the latter grow on the professional path. In the same time, he is the one who offers the practical assistance in order to ensure the possibility of attaining the professional and personal development objectives. Thus, the *mentor* possesses the necessary professional and skill knowledge to fulfill the tasks of that position successfully. Mentoring—as a socio-human activity—has its roots in the United States of America, having been applied initially in economy and industry in the first half of the twentieth century. Noticing the results obtained, the method was taken and adapted in business, management, and education.

It is well known that, when a novice teacher is hired in a school, he makes great effort to comprise and adapt to the organizational environment and existing rules and regulations. But this process could be straightforward if there were a special mentoring program within the school, with the help of which the new teacher would be offered—for a certain period of time—special attention. Thus, he would integrate into the organizational culture; he would develop the necessary skills more rapidly and would form the abilities that are specific to his position. Not least, through this kind of program, his relation-building process with the other members of organization would be facilitated. In this context, the roles of coach and mentor are so important in the professional life of any person.

According to David Clutterbuck, the mentor is a humble, wise person, interested in helping other people and has the capacity of not asserting his authority. Although mentoring is focused on asking questions, this does not mean that the mentor cannot offer advice, even if in a guarded manner. "The mentor has a double role: he has to challenge and support in the same time. He has to be the person who will not let you give up that easily." wrote Clutterbuck, specifying that sincerity is mandatory in mentoring ("Harnessing the Power of Mentoring," David Clutterbuck, October 2012).

7.2.1 *The Characteristics of a Mentor*

A successful mentor is characterized as a:

Supportive Person A mentor is the person who cares for the novice's needs and aspirations. This attitude of offering help is essential for the successful development of the novice. A mentor has to encourage the volunteer to accept the challenges and overcome the difficulties.

Patient Person The mentor is patient and willing to spend time in order to achieve the mentoring responsibilities. A mentor secures enough time in his timetable for the interaction with the novice. The necessary period of time for the meetings is set together by the two people: the mentor and the novice.

Respected Person A mentor is a person who has already gained the respect of his colleagues in the organization, in his community, and in his professional circle.

People-Oriented Person A mentor is a person who is truly interested in other people and wishes to help others. The successful mentor is someone with "good people skills," who knows how to communicate efficiently and listen actively. The mentor also has to be able to solve disputes and offer the adequate feedback.

Good Motivator A mentor is someone who inspires the mentored person to become better. The mentor has to know how to motivate through encouragement, feedback, and support given to the mentored in challenging tasks (as the case may be).

Efficient Teacher A mentor has to know very well the abilities that the mentored has to possess at work and be able to teach the volunteer these abilities efficiently. A mentor has to watch and organize the learning process of the volunteer. In other words, the mentor has to identify and use any opportunity for the learning purposes of the volunteer.

Confident A mentor has to be confident in his career so that he can sincerely express his pride in the results of the mentored. A mentor should appreciate the abilities and strengths of the volunteer without considering his achievements a threat for him. The mentor who is confident about his place and his position will enjoy every success of the volunteer and will be able to rejoice in every stage of his development process.

In the research published by British researchers regarding the profile of an efficient mentor, they include the following qualities:

- Experience and ability to organize
- Knowledge of reality, of practical applicability, of restraints
- People skills
- Ability to know when to step in
- Lessons management
- Diverse practical ideas that make a lesson coherent
- Methods of class organization
- Knowledge of developing skills in class
- Ability to handle different situations
- The qualification to transform academic information into lesson content that is comprehensible to the students
- Aptitude regarding the graduation of activities
- Timing
- Different ways to react to the students' attempts to disturb the class
- The continuous awareness regarding the events taking place and the possibility to change the course of action instantly when necessary
- The ability to deal any situation
- Ways of interpreting events and of reacting accordingly
- Knowledge of assessment and grading
- Differential treatment of students
- Knowledge regarding the course of a lesson

7.3 The Mentoring Process

In the relevant literature, there are numerous definitions given to the mentoring process; what is important is that mentoring be perceived as a process whose objective is to transmit information and shape a set of abilities, organized by highly experienced people in a certain area and oriented to novices. For this reason, mentoring must be considered as an interactive process between two people, based on the premise of both parties involvement, of guiding the learning development and assuming the obligations coming to them according to their statuses.

Any mentoring relationship developing within an organization takes place over a period of time that is enough for the mentor to ensure that the mentored develops and richly uses the information given. And, because over this period of time, both the needs and the nature of the relationship change, the mentor has to be the one aware of these changes, and he must vary—according to the demands—the degree and type of attention, help, advice, information, and encouragement offered.

The mentoring process is not a continuous one, but develops over a fixed period of time, aiming to attain preset objectives (that belong both to the mentor and the mentored). Between the mentor and the trainee, there is a relationship focused on finality, which lies in the optimal assimilation and usage of necessary knowledge and abilities for that position.

The mentoring process is an arduous one but essential for the trainees and novices. Within school context, a mentor is an experienced teacher, involved in supporting a novice teacher in the teaching staff.

The comprehensive initiation of fresh teachers who need guidance and help for adjusting to the new culture is more than a necessity. The majority of fresh teachers have not yet experienced the benefits of a mentoring program. Schools should be different, inviting, and particularly open to offer support to fresh teachers. Initiation includes all the activities through which fresh teachers are prepared and encouraged to get to know the mission and philosophy of the school, thus realizing that they are part of the same team.

The necessity of mentoring is supported and promoted by many experienced teachers, who believe that implementing a mentoring program in schools is important (Ingersoll & Kralik, 2004). A major role in mentoring is detained by the school masters and the department heads that need to observe the recently come teachers periodically, to talk to them and correct when and where it is necessary, teach them, and offer resources, books, files, and anything helpful.

It would be ideal if schools become real *acculturation* areas where the young teachers feel welcome, accepted, and supported until they are able to conduct both the class of students and the contents taught. Thus, a mentoring program designed according to the specificities of each school should exist. Each school is unique, so it is important that from the beginning, the novice teachers would be helped to deal with the troublesome cultural context of the new school community.

There is a necessity for new teachers to be integrated as soon as possible, as this would be optimal for the organization. One can also resort to companies specialized in personal training, the drawback being the financial aspect (often such programs have high prices). Domestic mentoring programs are also adequate for the situations in which a training program is not on the market or when training sessions need to be quickly implemented.

Christian schools—James Drexler believes—should be the head of strong relationships and community. An essential way to achieve this ideal is to ensure our intern teachers are supported and built in such a way that each of them can become an efficient educator. Obviously, the intern teachers need opportunities to grow professionally, to improve their skills and learn from mistakes and work in contexts that inspire trust and encouragement beside their colleagues, in order to develop as teachers. Unfortunately, the majority of intern teachers only receive their books and curriculum; they are shown the classrooms; they are burdened with various preparation sessions, many students, and responsibilities and are offered support only symbolically, at best. We are not surprised when we hear that numerous intern teachers abandon their profession. In the same time, the experienced teachers also need to develop, to perfect in their area, and, together with the intern teachers, to improve in active learning professional communities that result in stronger and more qualitative schools with high learning standards for students. *We can develop better activities in the Christian schools. We have to do it* (Drexler, 2015).

Another definition for mentoring: mentoring is "the significant contribution given by a person to another in order to help the other's transition in terms of knowledge, professional experience, and thought" (Megginson and Clutterbuck, 1995, p. 13).

For this reason, a mentor supports a person during a transition process that requires additional effort, such as a major change in personal circumstances, career, or development. The person receiving the help is often called a "scholar" or "the one who learns." Mentoring is just one of the supporting ways and one of the many possibilities in which the interns could be helped, for example, by their colleagues (colleague-to-colleague is peer support), managers, counselor, tutors/teachers and groups participating in learning groups or work teams, friends, or parents. An intern can benefit from various support ways, and, for various reasons, he can have more than one mentor at a certain point in time and can benefit from various kinds of support, according to the period of time that he finds himself. The traditional way of mentoring is one-to-one, but there are also other mentoring patterns as co-mentoring and group mentoring.

The mentoring relationship can be initiated by volunteers and can develop informally, when an individual seeks advice and support in another person. Mentoring can develop inside or outside an organization. In the majority of cases, people do not admit they actually have a mentor presently or they have benefitted from mentoring.

The above is associated to the reality that fresh teachers are adults, so that mentoring, initiation, and professional development plans have to be elaborated in the perspective of *andragogy*, "the method and practice of teaching adult learners." According to Malcolm Knowles (1980), the father of andragogy, the adult learning process is different from the children, so at least four important principles have to be taken into consideration:

- Adults need to know why they learn or do something and the way it will affect them directly.
- Adults bring their own life experience which should be used as resource for continuous learning.
- Adults are inclined to learn in a participatory way (solving problems rather than learning by heart).
- Adults want and need to apply the new input immediately.

Mentoring is a powerful instrument; it is ideal when we want to help people grow or when they find themselves in a transition time. This is the answer given by teacher David Clutterbuck to the question: "What is in fact mentoring?" And, to enlarge the perspective a little, I would like to add here other definitions which Clutterbuck, a global authority in mentoring area, has elaborated during the event "Harnessing the Power of Mentoring," organized by ITOL, on 18 October 2012:

- Mentoring implies the transition from the mechanical process to human process. Mentoring implies learning.
- Mentoring is a process that helps people think more thoroughly and more efficiently regarding their development as people, as professionals.

- Mentoring does not solve everything. It is not a solution that works indefinitely, but it meets a specific need.
- Mentoring is based on asking difficult and uncomfortable questions.

7.4 The Stages of Mentoring Process

The stages of mentoring are landmarks that need to be known by both of the actors in the mentoring relationship. As guidance, help, and respect favoring personal and professional development and the knowledge and generational competence transfer, mentoring is based on the interpersonal relationship between the mentor and the intern.

The relevant literature describes various mentoring patterns.

Lois Zachary considers mentoring as a four-stage learning cycle:

Stage 1: Preparing the mentoring relationship.
Stage 2: Negotiation stage, establishing partnership agreements for the future relationship.
Stage 3: Developing the mentoring relationship, activating growth and development, and easing the learning process.
Stage 4: Ending the mentoring relationship and preparing the separation.

Hamilton and Mocket accept the following stages:

Stage 1 – Creating a trustworthy connection, implying:

- The knowledge and creation of a communicative relationship
- Identification and understanding the differences
- Planning the first meetings

Stage 2 – Exploring the possibilities consisting in:

- Defining the objectives of the action
- Choosing the activities or subjects of mentoring meetings

Stage 3 – Ascertaining limits through:

- The knowledge of own limits
- Updating the commitments
- Seeking exterior support and taking the counsel of other colleagues

Stage 4 – The end of mentoring cycle and the beginning of another cycle, which concerns:

- Turning the results to advantage
- Establishing the mentoring impact in the professional life
- Continuing or ending the mentoring relation

7.5 Values and Principles Underlying Mentoring

The mentoring process is based on the following values and principles:

- Admitting that people have good intentions (Hay, 1995).
- We admit that people can change and develop (Hay, 1995).
- Knowledge of the individual's learning style.
- Admitting the fact that there are differences among individuals.
- Personal and professional development is necessary so that a person can become successful.
- Encouraging individuals to develop.
- Developing competence.
- Encouraging the cooperation, not the competition.
- The thinking that is oriented toward the future and the development of the ability to transfer and apply the assimilated input into new situations.
- Equal opportunities in the organization.
- Stimulating the analysis.
- Seeking new ideas, theories, and knowledge.
- Meditating over the past experiences as a way to understand and learn.
- Appreciating the fact that we are the ones to create the mentoring meaning the way we want it (Hay, 1995; Jowett, Shaw, & Tarbitt, 1997).

7.6 Conclusions

The role of mentoring is vital both in terms of observation and of analysis, offering the central focus during the practical activity. The intern teachers need opportunities for development and maturation through a professional development plan well structured, comprehensive, and scholarly at the beginning of the career.

To conclude, any organization will run more efficiently and lower expenses for instruction if it has particularly prepared people in order to become mentors or trainers for certain situations. These people are experienced in their career who want to share their knowledge and are counselors who guide the employees emotionally, professionally, and morally. Mentors and trainers periodically offer specific feedback on the performance of the person they train. Also, they are authentic information and help sources in obtaining easiness, being in fact models. Mentoring is a powerful instrument, optimal when we want to help people grow or when they find themselves in a transition.

References

An International Perspective. Johannesburg: Butterworth-Heinemann.
Available: http://www.3creek.com (2004, July 3).

Drexler, J. L. (2011). *Nurturing the school community: Teacher induction and professional learning communities*. Colorado Springs, CO.
Drexler, J. (2015). *Nurturing the school community*. Budapest: FotoGOLD Printing house.
Hay, J. (1995). *Transformational mentoring*. McGraw-Hill Book Company.
Ingersoll, R., & Kralik, J. (2004). *The impact of mentoring on teacher retention: What the research says*.
Jowett, J. V., Shaw, E. D., & Tarbitt, V. (1997). *A guide to mentoring. Leeds Metropolitan University*.
Knowles, M. S. (1980). *The modern practice of adult education: From pedagogy to andragogy*. Englewood Cliffs, NJ: Prentice Hall/Cambridge.
Megginson, D., & Clutterbuck, D. (1995). *Mentoring in action: A practical guide for managers*.
Methodologies and innovative mentoring and coaching strategies to prevent dumping of teachers teaching career debutants – LLP-LDV/VETPRO/2013/R0/353, financed by the European Commission, 2014.

Chapter 8
Recruitment and Selection of Human Resources in the Romanian Organizations

Alexandra Florina Beiu

Abstract Man sits in the center of all business. All other resources, land, buildings, mechanisms, equipment, vehicles, or money, are only of secondary importance. Without people, there cannot be business. Businesses have no other purpose than to serve the people's needs. Of course, people have different roles within a business and have many links with other businesses. People are employees of a business. Sometimes they are its managers; other times they are suppliers, customers, creditors, debtors, and shareholders. Frequently, however, they may have all these attributes together. For markets require effective management practice and performance at all levels, and this cannot be achieved without competent human resources and highly motivated performance. For any successful organization, human resources is the core around which all other resources revolve (material, financial, informational), and issues concerning recruitment, selection, training, development, evaluation, reward, and motivation are the main research directions of human resource management of any organization. In these conditions, a survey was conducted on the recruitment and selection of human resources in Romanian organizations.

Keywords Recruitment • Selection • Human resources • Recruitment sources • Methods of recruitment

8.1 Introduction

Human resource management will include and will increase in all domains of the economic, social, political, and cultural specter. It is obvious that the manager responsible must have a great capacity for analysis and synthesis, mobility and flexibility in thinking, negotiating capacity, availability of dialogue, and teamwork, above all, to know how to motivate employees in obtaining good results and to

A.F. Beiu (✉)
Bucharest Academy of Economic Studies, Bucharest, Romania
e-mail: alexbeiu@yahoo.com

S. Văduva et al. (eds.), *Solutions for Business, Culture and Religion in Eastern Europe and Beyond*, DOI 10.1007/978-3-319-63369-5_8

realize that success can only be achieved when every employee feels that it is valuable and it is important in the organization.

In any organization, a time of personal change can intervene. If work extends, that will require an additional number of employees. In addition, some employees leave the organization for various reasons; others are promoted, transferred, retired, or fired. All these mutations create vacancies. Department staff has the responsibility to plan human resources necessary to the organization and, in terms of this, to draw up concrete plans for recruitment and selection. Ultimately, the purpose of any recruitment and selection process is finding the right man for a particular position. If at first glance this seems like a simple activity, things are more complex because in choosing suitable staff there are numerous possibilities of making some bad decisions.

8.2 The Need for Human Resources Recruitment Activity

Recruitment is the search activity and the attraction within the organization, of a group of interested and capable persons, which have the ability to fill vacancies by choosing candidates for these positions accordingly (Mănăilă, Petcu, & Mihăiță, 2004a).

Organizations in general and businesses in particular to survive, it must properly resolve these problems:

- Identify the skills and the choice or selection of candidates corresponding requirements better new or vacant positions
- Identifying and attracting competitive candidates using the most appropriate methods, resources, or methods of recruitment

Solving these problems means the success is favorable to the entire staffing process, a process important in the economy of companies considering the effects of possible mistakes or errors of employment.

Thus, before taking the decision for the employment of new claimants, it is necessary to verify the reality of recruitment and the need to take into account the possibility of achieving other alternatives. Specifically, if a job exists, it does not mean that there must be; if the post remained vacant, it is possible to disband. It can decide the transfer of tasks to another job or vacancy can be maintained when changing some circumstances.

Therefore, recruiting human resources refers to the confirmation of the need to hire personnel to some changes in the employment situation of personnel and actions of locating and identifying potential candidates and to attract the competitive, able to carry more efficient job requirements.

From this perspective, the recruitment needs can be strategic, because responding to long-term needs can respond to urgent requests for temporary or circumstantial or may be related to internal staff movements (promotion, transfers, developments).

Recruitment can be permanent and can only be done systematically or when a particular need arises. If human resources recruitment is conducted continuously and systematically, then the organization has the advantage of maintaining a permanent contact with the labor market.

Also, recruiting human resources can be spontaneous when individuals are turning to an organization, or caused, when the organization wants to occupy a certain position.

The character of spontaneity is manifested in situations where a large number of candidates who apply express their desire for employment to certain companies which have a high activity, even when the level of those organizations do not seem like opportunities for employment. Staff recruitment is the process of searching, tracking, identifying, and attracting potential candidates, from which a person can be chosen, this candidate presenting the professional characteristics necessary to best meet the requirements of existing and future vacancies.

Recruitment of human resource management is the process of maintaining and developing the most appropriate internal and external sources necessary to ensure competitive personnel that can achieve organizational goals. From this point of view, the recruitment process can be an asset, especially when the organization aims at maintaining or preserving links or contacts to external sources of recruitment. So, the organization tries to maintain a network of qualified applicants or potential applicants, even if there is not currently a vacancy or if the organization is in a period of downsizing (Manolescu, Lefter, & Deaconu, 2007a).

8.3 Recruitment Activity Base Staffing Process

In the opinion of specialists in human resources, for example, David J. Cherrington, staffing an organization, usually called employment, includes several core activities, namely, human resource planning, recruitment, and the selection of staff.

Other specialists in human resources believe in a concept like this (Klatt, Murdick, & Schuster, 1985), suggesting that the process of staffing within or outside the organization can be viewed as a sequence of specific human resource activities absolutely needed to achieve individual and organizational goals.

Thus, the process of staffing within the organization includes recruitment, selection, orientation, and integration of staff, while staffing within the organization requires some transfers, promotions, retraining, redeployment, development, etc., and possible retirements, resignations, redundancy, or death.

Recruitment logically follows human resource planning, as it aims to identify and attracting candidates for the replenishment net competitive and additional personal needs.

This means that the recruitment effort of an organization and the methods used are dependent on the planning of human resources and the specific posts to be filled (Manolescu, Lefter, & Deaconu, 2007b).

A similar view is expressed by other specialists in human resources, for example, Byars and Rue (1987), which emphasize the relationship between job analysis, personnel planning, recruitment, and selection of human resources (Fig. 8.1).

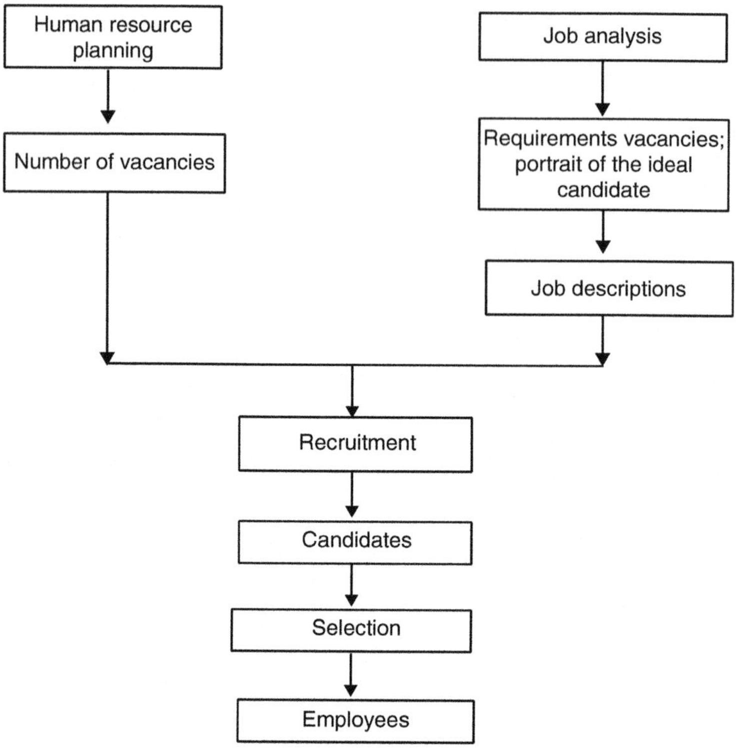

Fig. 8.1 Relations between job analysis, personnel planning, recruitment, and selection (Mănăilă, Petcu, & Mihăiță, 2004b)

According to the above, recruitment is generally the first contact between those who employ and those who are looking for a job, this also being a public activity. Also, employment is more than a simple business market, this being a long-term relationship particularly complex and many issues where stakeholders are concerned to avoid entering into a relationship with a partner inappropriate to build and maintain an advantageous relationship.

8.4 The Particularity of the Recruitment Process

Managerial practice in human resources proves (Milkovich & Boudreau, 2007), however, that mistakes can be made in the employment interview or the negotiation initiated by the employer and candidates due to numerous circumstances that may change the value of employment for any of the two parties.

Therefore, recruitment personality syndrome is a two-way process of communication between different organizations and individuals, in which both the organization or their representatives and candidates transmit signals related to the employment relationship in order to achieve the necessary comparison between the interests of both sides. The organization wants to send signals regarding its image and reputation, suggesting the opportunities it has to offer, the fact that it is a good place to work, but the company also wants to receive signals from candidates, so they can make a realistic evaluation of their potential.

The organization embodies the interests of the company and seeks to provide that information to potential candidates, tempting or persuading them to accept different positions. On the other hand, representatives of the organization assess the strengths and weaknesses of the candidates.

Candidates, in turn, want to transmit signals to suggest that they are the applicants most suitable or most competitive and must receive job offers for employment. Successful candidates are methodical, well prepared, and well organized, interested in finding a job, and also prepared to sacrifice time and effort.

On the other hand, candidates who offer their capabilities, attitudes, skills, qualifications, or experience and desire to work in the organization are trying to convince that it is necessary to be provided with the most complete and accurate information in order to decide on employment relationship.

Decision to accept a job is influenced by three main factors (Constantinescu et al., 1999):

1. Objective factors: salary, nature of work, location, opportunities for advancement; therefore, it is necessary to identify those aspects that are attractive to a job candidate. This means that recruitment must be regarded as a marketing activity.
2. Subjective factors: there are opinions that people are drawn to organizations whose images match their personality.
3. Recruitment factors: since most candidates lack sufficient knowledge about the job or the organization where job opportunities are likely to be influenced by a recruitment specialist.

A special importance is the realism of data and information that must be based on the opinions of both its employees and organization-specific conditions in comparison to those offered by competing organizations in order to determine the pull factor for potential candidates.

If the candidate misunderstands the nature of the work or the organization, the effects will be as serious as if the employer misunderstands the candidate. There is always a confrontation of expectation with reality.

Because of this, it is desirable that in the recruitment process, a partnership between specialist recruiters and potential candidate be adopted, for the benefit of both parties.

8.5 Policies and Strategies for Recruitment

A particularly important stage in the process of recruitment is the development of strategies and recruitment policies that establishes objectives or designates concepts, code of conduct for the organization in the field of recruitment and conducts specific activities, and overall attitudes, intentions, and guidelines for recruitment.

Also, recruitment strategies and policies define how the organization fulfills its responsibilities in staff recruitment, as well as the philosophy and values of the organization relating to this process. Because organizational policies have a significant impact on the effectiveness of the recruitment process, in many situations it is necessary for general policies to be understood and interpreted appropriately, in order to achieve the most appropriate support for these policies.

8.6 Sources of Recruitment

Identifying sources of recruitment is an important step in the course of recruitment sources, which can be internal or external, but most organizations use both sources, increasing the chances to discover and attract candidates as competitive.

To fill vacancies represents an analysis of the advantages and disadvantages that presents each recruitment source to which it appeals.

8.6.1 Advantages and Disadvantages of Internal Recruitment Sources

In the case of internal recruitment, this does not constitute a proper job, but more along the lines of a job change, which involves the same steps as internal and external candidates. Potential problems that may occur:

- Internal recruitment is not always possible, especially if the organization is developing rapidly or has not conducted a proper training of their employees so they can take over new responsibilities.
- If there is a certain stagnation or amplification routine, habit, it is possible that internal recruitment is not the most appropriate method.
- For geographically dispersed organizations, the access to certain levels or the encouragement of transfers from one place to another is a particular problem.
- Promoting a mediocre employee in a higher post.

Advantages of internal recruitment:

- Organizations know better the "strengths" and "weaknesses" of the candidates.
- It can attract candidates much easier.

- The selection is much faster and more efficient.
- It allows only the specific qualification of the organization just by recruiting a candidate from its frame.
- The likelihood of inappropriate decisions is much diminished.
- The timing of guidance and mentoring of new employees is greatly diminished.

The disadvantages of internal recruitment:

- It prevents the infusion of "fresh air" and discourages the promotion of new ideas.
- It favors the manifestation of Peter's principle, according to which people tend to get up the corporate ladder, by rising up to their level of incompetence.
- It can show favoritism or trigger numerous conflicts or emotional states determined by how different the perception of facts or circumstances regarding the promotion of employees is viewed within the company.
- I can challenge the occurrence of vacancies in the chain, the so-called ripple effect of vacancy.

8.6.2 Advantages and Disadvantages of External Recruitment

Upon regarding that vacancies cannot be filled from domestic sources, it is necessary to act outside the organization to identify possible external sources.

Advantages of external recruitment of staff:

- It helps identify and attract a greater number of potential candidates.
- It helps improve the recruitment process itself because of the possibility offered to compare internal and external candidates.
- It enriches the organization's internal human potential and eliminates possible stagnation or routines installed.
- It allows the reduction of costs or staff training costs.

Disadvantages of external recruitment:

- Identifying, attracting, and assessing candidates are made more difficult, just based on references or some short interviews.
- The risk of hiring candidates who subsequently prove they cannot maintain the high potential that they have shown during the selection process.
- The cost of recruiting staff is much higher.

8.6.2.1 Stages and Methods of Human Resource Recruitment

Human resources recruitment requires compliance with stages:

1. Budgeting affected recruitment activity is highlighted in all categories of expenses that may involve the recruitment: wages, the cost of consumables, the cost of recruitment sources, and the cost of job advertisements.

2. Establishing responsibilities for recruiting human resources, they can return to specialized companies (recruiters or human resources consultancy).
3. Analyzing the company's human resource plan, this providing information on the human resources and the categories of employees that the company needs.
4. Identifying and analyzing specifications of vacant posts mentioned in the job and analyzing conditions which potential candidates must meet in order to fill those positions.
5. Analyzing the labor market is important because it may show some information regarding the situation of labor supply.
6. Identifying and recruiting source election, significantly influencing the level of costs, while the menus of this work and the work of the entire company as extension of recruitment or lack of productivity mean low productivity level vacancies, which means reducing efficient company activity

   The main criteria according to which recruitment sources can be identified and selected are:

   (a) Costs
   (b) The number of candidates to be recruited
   (c) The time in which candidates can be recruited
   (d) The nature and complexity of vacancies
   (e) The size of the company

7. Establishing the recruitment period that should take into account the organization's human resources' needs, from those that the company may use for the availability of candidates and the budget allocated to this activity.
8. The forming and noticing of employment choice at this stage are designed job advertisements, in terms of content, form, and dimensions. The type of advertisement should also be chosen, depending on the communication channel through which it is transmitted: press, radio, television, and the Internet.
9. Electing the means of transmission or communication of the employment notice, this step being conditioned by the nature and complexity of the job for which published employment is offered, by its content and form notice of employment, and the cost of each method of transmission.
10. Impacting assessment, expressing efficiency recruitment action.
11. Cost assessing the recruitment company, due to the fact that budgeting affects the recruiting activity, which includes a series of charges arising out of this activity.

8.6.2.2 Human Resources Recruitment Methods

Information and knowledge on previous similar recruitment processes can serve to better understand the importance and diversity of human resource recruitment methods that a company can use in order to cover the necessary human resources.

Overall, the most used methods of recruitment of human resources, which can be found at the level of the various organizations, are:

- Employment ads
- Direct contracts
- Collaboration with recruitment of human resources
- Promotion
- Transfers
- Rehiring
- Recommendations
- Recruiting online
- Participation in job fairs
- Using your own database

  – Employment ads

It is the most popular method of identifying, locating, searching, and attracting candidates to fill a vacancy. Employment or recruitment notice can be used to recruit candidates from several sources: press, television, radio, the Internet, and job fairs.

- Direct contacts

Direct contacts are one way of recruiting candidates that is a little expensive, because those who are looking for a job at the company have to travel in order to obtain information about the availability of jobs. The advantage is that the company recruits without making any effort.

- Collaboration with recruitment agencies

This entails a partnership or cooperation, based on a service contract, for an organization that wishes to hire staff and agency. The advantage is a large number of candidates in a relatively short time, the main drawback being linked to the high cost of this method.

- Promotion

This is the most used method, the advancement of an employee to a higher post in terms of work or pay level.

- Transfers

This relates to the transfer of employees from different branches, outlets, or production centers or other activities of the company at its headquarters.

- Reengagement

Consists of rehiring former employees of the company, to cover its human resource needs.

- Recommendations

It is a method that is based on the suggestions of parents, current or former employees, about particular candidates that could potentially fill vacant posts.

- Recruiting online

Recruiting online is based on Internet use and notice of employment. The essence of this method is to publish job advertisements on the Internet. This can be achieved by concluding a collaboration with one or more companies administering the sites for recruiting human resources in exchange for fees or publishing actual job advertisements on the website of the company.

- Participation in job fairs

This method consists in presenting the organization employment offers during job fairs, where companies have direct contact with candidates and get their applications.

8.7 The Selection of Human Resources

The selection of human resources is one of the basic activities of human resource management, which is usually done within the human resource department, but the responsibility falls on the managers from different hierarchical levels.

Organizations in general and businesses in particular have always been concerned about recruitment, because this activity can become very expensive if an employer hires persons who, ultimately, are regarded as improper for job requirements.

Personnel selection is the activity of human resource management, which consists of choosing, according to certain criteria, the most competitive and most suitable candidate to fill a particular post.

The main objective of personnel selection is to select those employees who are closest to the desired performance standards and who are most likely to achieve individual and organizational objectives.

According to the theory and practice in human resource management, staff selection process is conducted in several stages:

- Choice of preliminary candidates
- Filling out job application
- Interviewing for a job
- Testing for employment
- Checking references
- Medical examination
- Final interview
- Decision of employment
- Installation on the job

Most organizations generally reject at each stage of the selection process unwanted applicants, but some organizations allow all candidates to go through the whole process of selection. However, in practice, not everyone will always go through all stages of the selection process. There are situations in which, when the candidate turns out to possess the necessary qualities for a particular job requirement, this reduces the number of steps in the selection, sometimes even being hired after only the first interview.

Each stage of the recruitment process must be designed to obtain specific information, relevant and useful in choosing the candidate deemed most appropriate or as a basis for employment decisions.

Recruitment can be seen as a two-way communication process and as part of the organization's relationship with the external environment.

Therefore, to discuss the candidacy of a person in order to fill a specific vacancy, the organization needs a minimum of information about that particular person.

Job application may be accompanied by curriculum vitae, the more the candidate is required to submit a short biography detailing aspects of the intersessional to a possible employer, showing the main data of civil status, address, education, experience in job-specific business activity, job performance, previous positions, distinctions, etc.

Therefore, curriculum vitae is the starting point in any selection process, mediating, usually meeting between applicants and representatives of the organization and one of the means of the preliminary screening of candidates.

Also the curriculum vitae is regarded as one of the most practical methods of evaluation, based on biographical information. Therefore, it should be a concise document, attractive, and exciting in form and in content, to arouse the interest of those who read it to get to know the candidate, giving him a greater chance at the interview.

Personnel selection can:

- Empirical methods, which are based on imposed criteria, but on recommendations, impressions, and presentation to a discussion of the candidates and their appearance.
- Scientific methods are based on personal and scientific methods and use means or methods and techniques of personnel evaluation.

8.8 Methodology

Motivating employees is one of the major problems faced by each company. The principal data collection is structured based on a questionnaire.

8.8.1 Sample

Therefore, 502 persons were evaluated, both genders, holding management positions or positions of responsibility in society. The ages of the people were between 23 years and maximum 45 years.

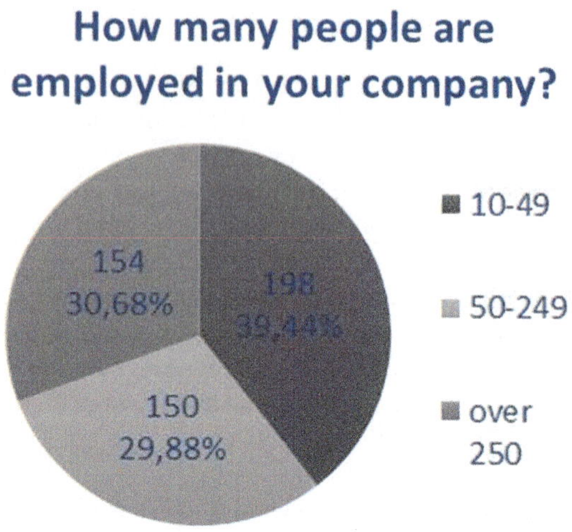

Fig. 8.2 How many people are employed in your company?

8.8.2 *Sampling Method Selection*

Sample size: 502 people in 41 counties, 15.7% of respondents working in commerce, 30.9% in manufacturing, and 38.8% in services.

Inclusiveness: the sample is representative of the collection represented with an error of ±4.9% at the limited probability of 95% guarantee.

8.8.3 *Data Analysis and Interpretation*

We can see that 198 people work in companies of medium size, 150 people work in large companies, and 154 people work in small size companies.

As we can see, the main activity is services with a rate of 38.8% from the respondents followed by industry 30.9% and commerce 15.7%.

The result of the analysis shows us that 42.89% of people were satisfied, 25.19% were very satisfied, and 21.45 were neither satisfied nor dissatisfied.

The highest share has people with a bachelor's degree, that means 240 people, followed by a master's degree and high school studies. The lowest share is the people with just gymnasium studies, 42 persons.

8.9 Conclusions

Achieving higher quality results in and increase of economic and social activity, but it requires an optimum use of all resources. Among these, a decisive component is the quality of the results decisively influencing economic activity. All management

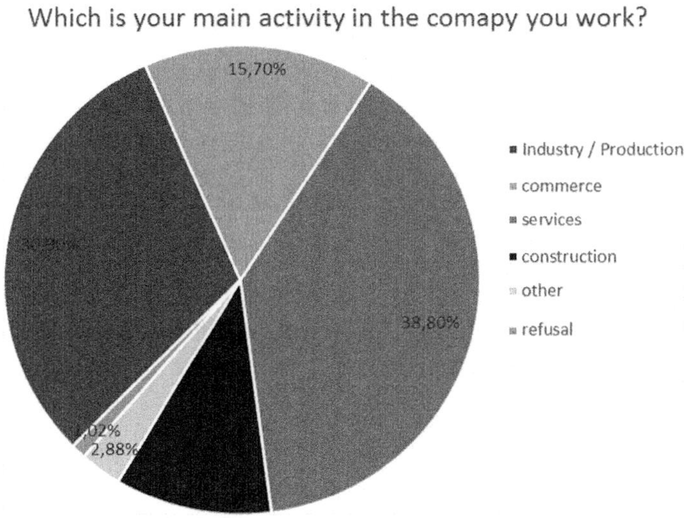

Fig. 8.3 Which is your main activity in the company you work?

functions are performed by people, driving business success or failure, depending on the assimilation of the art to work with people. The study contributes to the knowledge management process of the human behavior of people, human relations, and the use of methods and techniques that influence them.

Rational use of human resources is a basic condition for the success of an organization in performing their duties. This requires the concern of the leadership regarding the recruitment and selection of personnel, its judicious distribution on jobs, aspirations, and motivation to achieve their integration into the overall organizational objectives.

The conclusion is clear in regard to the search of job opportunities, meaning that everyone will have the chance to take a job only if they can demonstrate training, skills, and abilities needed to make a better offer. They must know how to highlight the best knowledge and skills they possess, to develop their own strategies to make themselves competitive.

Candidates are detained after recruitment and selection if they meet the criteria required by the vacancy and will have an important role in achieving success for the company.

Those who make hiring decisions believe that the choice is determined by future collaborations. This is why their decision should not be taken in haste, as it combines connection strategy and enterprise balance.

It is important that in the process of recruitment and selection of staff, the perfect principles and methods to be strictly followed are defined, if not the company will be threatened in the future by its very own operating system.

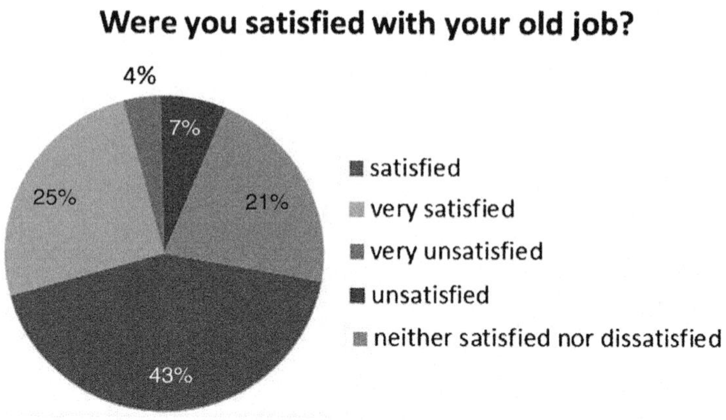

Fig. 8.4 Are you satisfied with your old job?

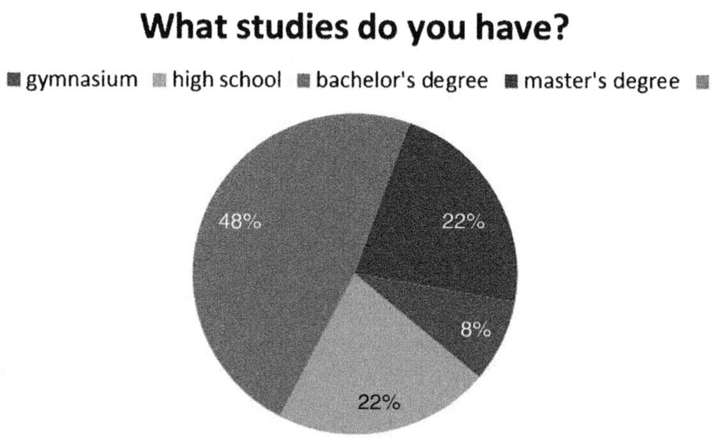

Fig. 8.5 What studies do you have?

In an organization, a predominant climate of unfavorable labor will result in low efficiency of work, a high grade of disciplinary violations, and a high turnover of staff.

Companies benefit from an extensive array of ways in recruiting, from employee recommendations to signs posted on online forums frequented by certain categories of professionals.

The recruitment and selection of specific methods were used, which was taken into account so that the activity of companies and the employment of personnel through job description and through specific requirements would achieve the social objectives at all levels of its organization.

A manager attaches great importance to communication with staff. Thus, it can resolve important issues related to business activities, problems, or employee complaints within the organization.

References

Byars, L. L., & Rue, L. W. (1987). *Human resource management* (p. 135). Edition Homewood Irwin.

Constantinescu, D. A., şi colab. (1999). *Managementul resurselor umane* (pp. 116–117). Bucureşti: Colecţia Naţională.

Klatt, L. A., Murdick, R. G., & Schuster, F. E. (1985). *Human resource management* (p. 171). Columbus, Toronto, London, Sydney: Charles E. Merrill Publishing, A Bell Howell Company.

Mănăilă, I., Petcu, M., & Mihăiţă, D. (2004a). *Consilier-Managementul Resurselor Umane* (p. R 35-002). Editura Rentro & Straton.

Mănăilă, I., Petcu, M., & Mihăiţă, D. (2004b). *Consilier- Managementul Resurselor Umane* (p. R 35-003). Editura Rentrop & Straton.

Manolescu, A., Lefter, V., & Deaconu, A. (2007a). *Managementul Resurselor Umane* (p. 270). Editura Economică.

Manolescu, A., Lefter, V., & Deaconu, A. (2007b). *Managementul Resurselor Umane* (p. 273). Editura Economică.

Milkovich, G. T., & Boudreau, J. W. (2007), op. Cit., p. 241.

Chapter 9
Identifying the Main Factors of Workplace Flexibility Among Romanian Employees

Viorel Lefter, Adriana AnaMaria Davidescu, and Ionut Casuneanu

Abstract Workplace flexibility gained increasingly more importance in the last decade, companies using it as a useful instrument to improve retention, to increase the overall level of work motivation and also to assure an adequate personal life to employees.

In this context, the paper aimed to identify the main flexibility factors among Romanian employees using as method of investigation, the principal component analysis based on a sample of 100 employees.

Analyzing the main forms of flexibility activities, the majority of the respondents consider teamwork and usage of information technology as primordial elements of flexibility.

The empirical results of the principal component analysis revealed that two main elements of flexibility are very important for Romanian employees-autonomy of work teams and working time flexibility.

Workplace flexibility is very important because employees will be more productive and more engaged in their work when there are able to balance the demands of work with other aspects of their lives.

The availability of a variety of flexible work arrangements can help employees also maximize work-family balance, which benefits both the employee and the employer.

V. Lefter, Ph.D.
Department of Management, Bucharest Academy of Economic Studies, Bucharest, Romania
e-mail: viorel@lefter.org

A.A. Davidescu, Ph.D. (✉)
Department of Statistics and Econometrics, Bucharest Academy of Economic Studies, Bucharest, Romania

Department of Labour Market Policies, Senior Researcher at National Research Institute for Labour and Social Protection, Bucharest, Romania
e-mail: adrianaalexandru@yahoo.com

I. Casuneanu, Ph.D.
Bucharest Academy of Economic Studies, Bucharest, Romania
e-mail: icasuneanu@gmail.com

S. Văduva et al. (eds.), *Solutions for Business, Culture and Religion in Eastern Europe and Beyond*, DOI 10.1007/978-3-319-63369-5_9

Keywords Workplace flexibility • Employee motivation • Survey • Romanian employees • Flexibility factors

9.1 Introduction

Workplace flexibility has been defined by Kossek and Thompson (2016, p. 1) in their chapter published in the *Oxford Handbook of Work and Family* as "a formal or informal agreement between an employer and employee to provide individual job control over flexibility in timing, location, amount or continuity in concert with non-work needs." According to the results of Matos and Galinsky (2014), about 81% of US employers permit their employees to modify the start and the end of the work program, while 67% of them allow employees to work from home.

Workplace flexibility has been used lately as a useful instrument to equilibrate the relation between work and personal life and also to improve the degree of retention of employees and also to control the workload. McNall, Masuda, and Nicklin (2010) and Baltes, Briggs, Huff, Wright, and Neuman (1999) demonstrated that flexible working hours could lead to an increase in job satisfaction, while Fynes and Storrie (1998) mentioned the reduction of absenteeism and stress and also the increase of the work motivation as positive consequences of workplace flexibility.

Chung and Tijdens (2012) and Jones and Jones (2011) refer part time, job sharing, shift work, overtime, or the long time leaves as components of flexibility at the workplace.

Pitt-Catsouphes and Matz-Costa (2008) analyzed the opinions of employees of different ages about their flexibility needs and also who this flexibility would be reflected in their work commitment, revealing that the highest impact of flexibility was determined for employees ages 45 and older.

The potential influence of workplace flexibility on the overall level of job satisfaction has been investigated by Origo and Pagani (2008), using the data from Eurobarometer survey revealing an even higher impact of functional flexibility on the intrinsic component of job satisfaction.

Noonan, Estes, and Glass (2007) tested the assumption according to which workplace flexibility affects child care and domestic labor, proving that mothers who work part-time have improved their domestic labor and child care.

Analyzing the main benefits that workplace flexibility could bring to employees, the decrease of stress level, increases of health, well-being, and also positive impacts on personal life could be mentioned (Casey & Chase, 2004), while among the benefits of employers, we can mention the possibility to retain a motivated and qualified workforce, to improve the objectives of the organizations, to improve productivity of their own employees, and also to hire talented individuals in the business (Kossek & Thompson, 2016).

In this context of an increasing importance of workplace flexibility impact on the overall level of motivation of employees, the paper aims to identify the main workplace flexibility factors that could impact the satisfaction of Romanian employees, using the principal component analysis as the method of investigation based on a sample of 100 Romanian employees.

9.2 Literature Review

Jeffrey Hill et al. (2008, p. 2) define the workplace flexibility as "the ability of workers to make choices influencing when, where, and for how long they engage in work-related tasks."

Sloan Center on Aging and Work at Boston College considers that "flexibility enables both individual and business needs to be met through making changes to the time (when), location (where) and manner (how) in which an employee works. Flexibility should be mutually beneficial to both the employer and employee and result in superior outcomes" (Aequus Partners, 2010).

Workplace flexibility could be seen as a win-win situation in which employers' objective is to have a qualified workforce and employees need to improve work-life balance.

Kossek and Michel (2011) and Kossek and Thompson (2015, p. 12) mentioned four types of workplace flexibility:

1. Flexibility in scheduling.
2. Flexibility in place/location.
3. Flexibility in the amount of work/workload and hours.
4. Flexibility in leave periods and career continuity.

Casuneanu (2013) identified four types of workplace flexibility: working time flexibility, contractual flexibility, functional flexibility, and wage flexibility.

Working time flexibility can be found in the following forms:

- Work with flexible working hours.
- Part-time work.
- Work in overtime.
- Work outside normal working hours.

Contractual flexibility can be found in various flexible contracts for hiring workers: temporary contracts, fixed-term contracts, and self-employed contracts.

Functional flexibility involves the employees' ability to occupy various positions depending on work needs to undertake tasks that are specific to each stage. In order to accomplish this type of flexibility, an important role is the training of employees, according to the training needs of the company and the working team autonomy who enables them to adjust the company to new changes.

Wage flexibility aims at reducing labor costs balancing the ratio "effort-reward" in correlation with performance unit, variations of production activities, and internal and external markets conjuncture. Consequently, the financial rewards will depend on the productivity of the company and also on the market demand.

Coenen and Kok (2014) analyzed the effects of teleworking and flexible schedule on the performance of a new product development team, proving that indeed teleworking positively contributed to the development of the new product and also increased the quality of product development.

Martínez-Sánchez, Pérez-Pérez, De-Luis-Carnicer, and Vela-Jiménez (2007) investigated the relationship between teleworking, workplace flexibility, and firm performance pointing out that there is a positive relationship between them in the case of Spanish companies.

Important results of different workplace flexibility types were obtained by the 2013 WorldatWork Survey highlighting that teleworking, part time, and flex time (start/stop times) are the most usual types of workplace flexibility used by more than 80% of the companies and larger firms tend to offer more flexibility options for their employees. Another important result concerns the high prevalence of flex time, more than 54% of the companies, choosing to offer to their workers this type of flexibility programs. Also one of the results of the survey pointed out the positive impact of flexible working hours on the overall level of motivation of employees.

Important outcomes have been provided also by the 2015 E&Y flexibility survey using a sample of 9700 employees from eight countries, revealing that flexibility at work has been mentioned after wage and benefits as an important motivational factor. Ranking countries regarding the level of flexibility, Germany was the country with the highest number of employees with flexible schedules, while China and Japan were at the opposite side. Another interesting result refers to the fact that the new generation of millennials most likely appreciates and valorizes more working flexibility.

9.3 Research Methodology

9.3.1 Data Collection

The study analyzed the population of employees who live in urban areas, who work in companies with at least ten employees (including autonomous administration and corporations), who have a management position (general manager, manager, department manager, supervisor), and who also have at least five subordinates.

The sample size included 100 employees from micro-, small-, medium-, and large-sized Romanian companies. The questionnaire has been applied on individual employee, 33% of those working in construction activities, 29% in the service area, 12% in the transportations, and the rest in other areas.

9.3.2 Variable Measurements

The designed questionnaire has three main sections. The first section presents information related to the company (company size, area of activity, amount of turnover, etc.). The second section is dedicated to job and wage satisfaction and also to flexibility factors.

Job satisfaction and wage satisfaction were measured using four-point Likert-type scale with responses ranging from very dissatisfied (1) to very satisfied (4). Flexibility factors were measured using a five-point Likert scale where 1 means total disagree and 5 means total agree. The last section of the questionnaire reveals demographic information (such as age, gender, years of service, years of service on the actual position, the number of subordinates, basic profession, salary).

9.4 Research Results

9.4.1 Sample Profile

Analyzing the sample, about 70% of them are male, who had been in their current position for 1–3 years. The respondents with the age between 21 and 35 years (45%) represent the most significant group. Almost 75% of the respondents have higher education. As regards seniority in the company, 45% of employees declared that they have more than 5 years of experience. About a third of respondents say that they have more than 5 years of experience in management positions. In terms of job seniority, 40% of respondents say that they have more than 5 years of experience on the job (Table 9.1).

9.4.2 Descriptive Analysis

Analyzing both job satisfaction and wage satisfaction, it is worth to mention that the overall level of job satisfaction was 3.71 pointing out an acceptable level of satisfaction. Regarding the level of wage satisfaction, the average wage satisfaction being 3.19, the Romanian employees are indifferent to and most satisfied with their wages. It is interesting to point out the fact that the level of satisfaction associated with financial incentives tends to be smaller compared with the overall level of satisfaction, revealing the importance of nonfinancial incentives (Table 9.2).

In our study, we used the following measures for work flexibility based on a five-point Likert scale with responses ranging from strongly disagree (1) to strongly agree (5) in order to quantify their impact on the overall level of job satisfaction, taking into account the study of Casuneanu (2013):

Table 9.1 Respondents' profile

	Frequency (n = 100) (%)
Gender	
Male	70
Female	30
Age	
Under 20 years	20
21–35 years	45
36–50 years	24
50–65 years	11
Educational level	
Vocational school	3
High school	21
Technical school	1
College	0
Company size	
Micro (1–9)	20
Small (10–49)	33
Medium (50–249)	28
Large (over 250 employees)	19
University	75
Length of time working in the company	
Under 1 year	16
1–3 years	24
3–5 years	15
5–10 years	28
Over 10 years	17
Management position	
Yes	35
No	65
Years in same position	
Under 1 year	19
1–3 years	26
3–5 years	15
5–10 years	29
Over 10 years	11

Table 9.2 Means and standard deviations for overall job satisfaction

	Total employees	
Variable	Mean	SD
Overall job satisfaction	3.71	0.64
Wage satisfaction	3.19	1.65

- *Working time flexibility* referring to flexible work arrangements (flexible work schedule, reduced hours (part-time work), alternative locations (working at home)), working outside normal working hours.
- Schedule flexibility has been found to be highly associated with job satisfaction. Employees who perceived to have more flexibility on the job reported better sleep, more exercise, and a healthier lifestyle in general than those employees who did not perceive the availability of flexibility.
- *Contractual flexibility* (temporary contracts, fixed-term contracts).
- *Functional flexibility* (employee trainings, working team autonomy).
- *Wage flexibility* (financial and nonfinancial rewards).

Regarding the distribution of employees from the sample by the type of contract presented in Fig. 9.1, we can mention that the majority of them have permanent contracts (full-time work), 88%, while only 4% of them declared that they have part-time permanent contracts.

Regarding the components of working time flexibility, only 52% of the respondents declared that they agree with a flexible work schedule, while only 16% of the respondents agree with working at home, and about 64% disagree with the idea of working outside normal working hours (in the weekend) (Fig. 9.2).

Regarding the functional flexibility, we can mention that the majority considers the autonomy of working teams very important and the training of employees as elements of working flexibility and factors of increasing job satisfaction (Fig. 9.3).

Almost 75% of respondents consider that wage flexibility is very important in increasing the employee job motivation (Fig. 9.4).

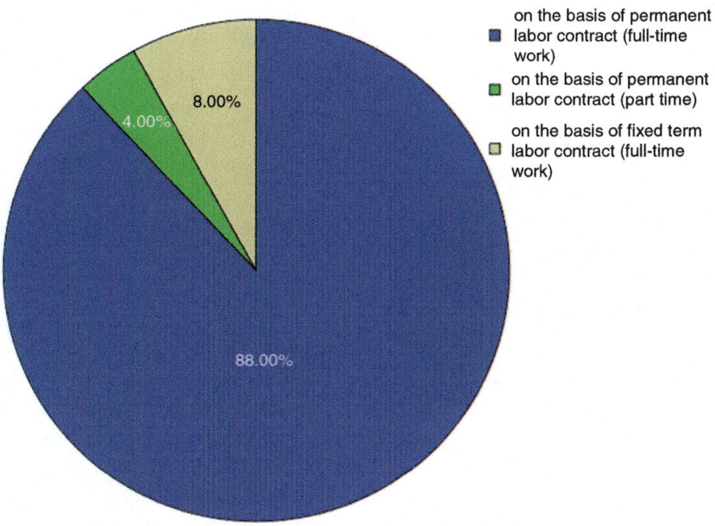

Fig. 9.1 The distribution of employees by type of contract

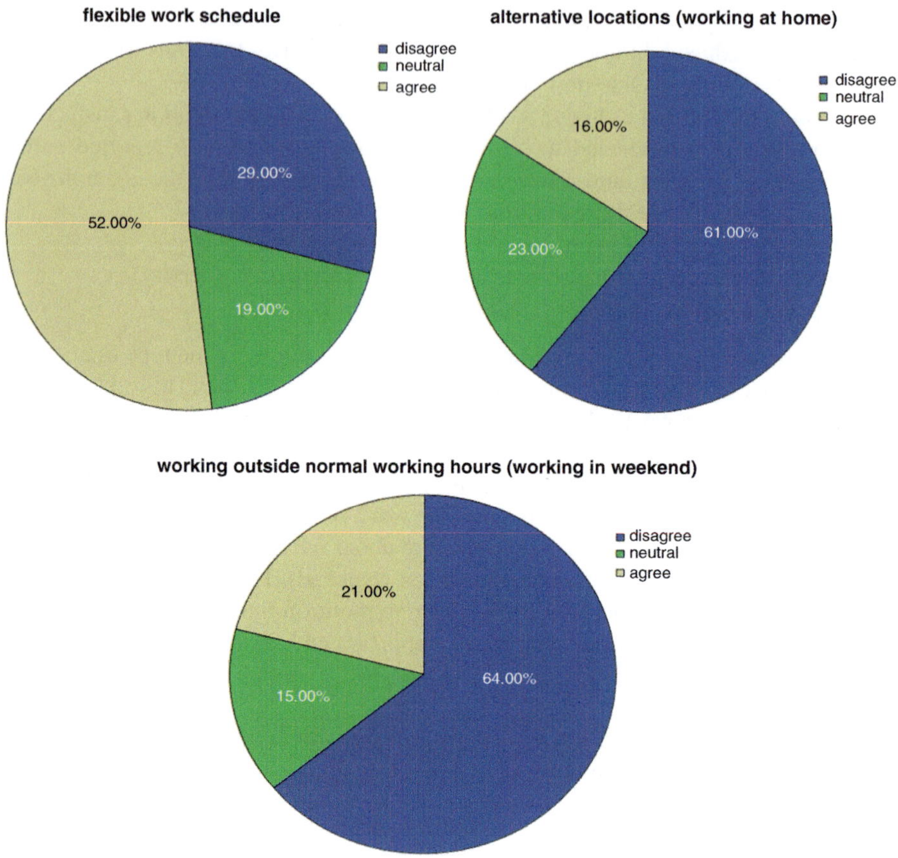

Fig. 9.2 The distribution of employees by working time flexibility

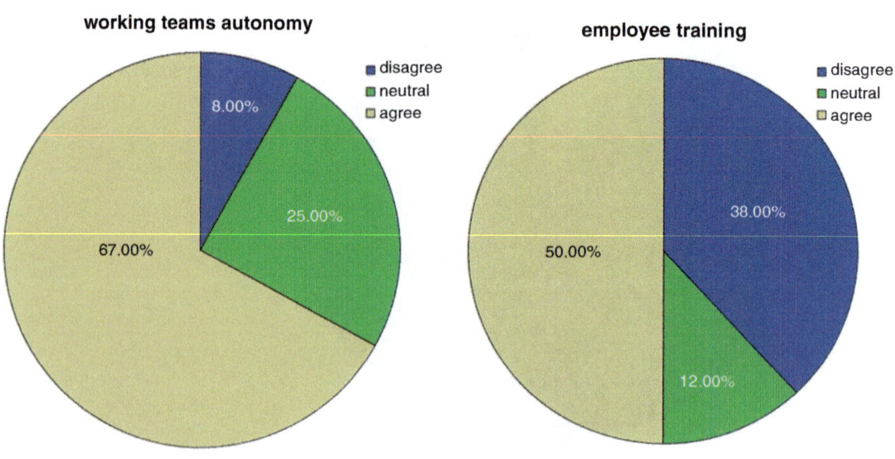

Fig. 9.3 The opinions of employees regarding the functional flexibility

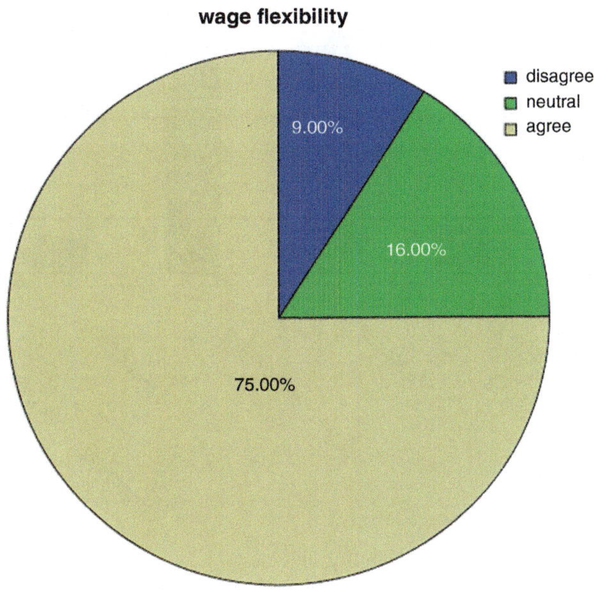

Fig. 9.4 The distribution of employees by wage flexibility

Table 9.3 Means and standard deviations for flexibility factors

	Mean	Std deviation
Employee training	3.29	1.533
Flexible work schedule	3.31	1.454
Alternative locations (working at home)	2.25	1.290
Working outside normal working hours (working in weekend)	2.24	1.280
Working teams autonomy	3.99	1.020
Wage flexibility	4.16	1.061

Regarding the main forms of flexibility activities, the majority of the respondents consider teamwork as a very important element and also the usage of information technology. At the opposite size, teleworking was mentioned to be the element with the lowest degree of flexibility (Fig. 9.5).

Mean scores for flexibility factors are presented in Table 9.3. The level of satisfaction for alternative locations or working outside normal working hours is low; thus the people are not very satisfied with this kind of flexibility option.

Correlations were calculated to describe the relationships between the flexibility factors (Table 9.4). The empirical results revealed low to moderate relationship between the variables.

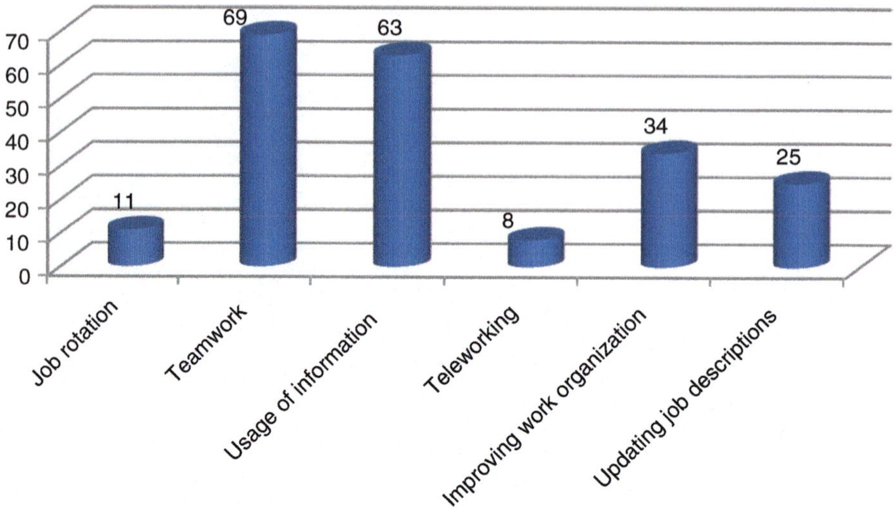

Fig. 9.5 Forms of flexibility activities

9.4.3 *The Principal Component Analysis of Flexibility Factors*

The main objective of the paper is to determine empirically the flexibility factors using the principal component analysis (PCA) with a positive impact to the overall level of satisfaction among the Romanian employees.

A principal component analysis (PCA) was conducted on the six items with oblique rotation (ProMax) using SPSS software. The Kaiser-Meyer-Olkin measure verified the sampling adequacy for analysis, KMO = 0.67, which is well above the acceptable limit of 0.5 (Field, 2009). Bartlett's test of sphericity indicated that correlations between items were sufficiently large for PCA (the probability is less than 1%).

KMO and Bartlett's Test		
Kaiser-Meyer-Olkin measure of sampling adequacy		0.677
Bartlett's test of sphericity	Approx. Chi-Square	82.283
	df	15
	Sig.	0.000

The empirical results of PCA revealed the existence of two principal components that explain 54.07% of the variance of the original variables selected by the rule of supra-unitary eigenvalues.

Table 9.5 presents the amount of variance explained by each component, revealing that the first principal component recovers almost 37.22% of the total variance, while the second component recovers another 16.84% of the total variance, both of them summing the value of 54% of total variance of the original variables.

Table 9.4 Relationships between flexibility factors

Correlation matrix[a]							
		Employee training	Flexible work schedule	Alternative locations (working at home)	Working outside normal working hours (working in weekend)	Working teams autonomy	Wage flexibility
Sig. (1-tailed)	Employee training		0.104	0.021	0.005	0.000	0.005
	Flexible work schedule	0.104		0.257	0.136	0.008	0.021
	Alternative locations (working at home)	0.021	0.257		0.010	0.061	0.005
	Working outside normal working hours(working in weekend)	0.005	0.136	0.010		0.034	0.006
	Working teams autonomy	0.000	0.008	0.061	0.034		0.000
	Wage flexibility	0.005	0.021	0.005	0.006	0.000	

[a]Determinant = 0.425

Table 9.5 Total variance explained

Component	Initial eigenvalues			Extraction sums of squared loadings			Rotation sums of squared loadings[a]
	Total	% of Variance	Cumulative %	Total	% of Variance	Cumulative %	Total
1	2.234	37.226	37.226	2.234	37.226	37.226	1.957
2	1.011	16.845	54.071	1.011	16.845	54.071	1.741
3	0.853	14.214	68.285				
4	0.797	13.285	81.569				
5	0.723	12.042	93.611				
6	0.383	6.389	100.000				

Extraction method: principal component analysis
[a]When components are correlated, sums of squared loadings cannot be added to obtain a total variance

Table 9.6 Pattern matrix[a]

	Component	
	1	2
Employee training	0.308	0.452
Flexible work schedule	0.744	−0.314
Alternative locations (working at home)	−0.149	0.791
Working outside normal working hours(working in weekend)	0.030	−0.716
Working teams autonomy	0.800	0.080
Wage flexibility	0.665	0.234

Extraction method: principal component analysis
Rotation method: Promax with Kaiser normalization
[a]Rotation converged in three iterations

In order to facilitate the interpretation of each component, it was recommendable to rotate the component matrix. Table 9.6 shows the factor loadings after the rotation. The items that cluster on the same components suggest that the first component can be interpreted in terms of working teams autonomy as the element of *functional flexibility* and the second one in terms of *working time flexibility* (working at home).

Autonomy enables work teams to adapt the organization of work in relation to changes that occur in organizations, and maybe the key of happiness at work is not the financial rewards or the money; it is the autonomy of employees and of the team, who will increase the quality of work. Working at home will allow employees to improve the balance of work-personal life by increasing the level of engagement in domestic labor and child care.

9.5 Conclusions

Workplace flexibility gained increasingly more importance in the last decade, companies using it as a useful instrument to improve retention, to increase the overall level of work motivation, and also to assure an adequate personal life to employees.

In this context, the paper aimed to identify the main flexibility factors among Romanian employees using as method the principal component analysis based on a sample of 100 employees.

Regarding the functional flexibility, we can mention that the majority considers the autonomy of working teams very important and the training of employees as elements of working flexibility and factors of increasing job satisfaction.

Regarding the main forms of flexibility activities, the majority of the respondents consider teamwork as a very important element and also the usage of information technology. At the opposite size, teleworking was mentioned to be the element with the lowest degree of flexibility.

The empirical results of the principal component analysis revealed that two main elements of flexibility are very important for Romanian employees—autonomy of work teams as proxy for functional flexibility and working time flexibility.

Autonomy enables work teams to adapt the organization of work in relation to changes that occur in organizations, and maybe the key of happiness at work is not the financial rewards or the money; it is the autonomy of employees and of the team, who will increase the quality of work. Working at home will allow employees to improve the balance of work-personal life by increasing the level of engagement in domestic labor and child care.

In conclusion, it is worth to mention that the opinions of Romanian employees are not so different from Europeans. They consider the workplace flexibility forms a useful tool for increasing productivity and engagement and also for creating equilibrium between their job and personal life.

References

Aequus Partners. (2010). Workplace flexibility: Advice, training, research. Retrieved October 6, 2010, from http://www.workplaceflexibility.com.au/index.htm

Baltes, B., Briggs, T. E., Huff, J. W., Wright, J. A., & Neuman, G. A. (1999). Flexible and compressed workweek schedules: A meta-analysis of their effects on work-related criteria. *Journal of Applied Psychology, 84*(4), 496–513. doi:10.1037/0021-9010.84.4.496.

Casey, J., & Chase, P. (2004). *Creating a culture of flexibility: What it is, why it matters, how to make it work Chestnut Hill*. Cambridge, MA: Boston College Center for Work and Family. Retrieved from http://www.bc.edu/centers/cwf/research/publications/meta-elements/pdf/BCCWFFlexibilityEBS.pdf.

Casuneanu, I. (2013). Îmbunătăţirea flexibilităţii forţei de muncă din întreprinderile româneşti folosind practicile în domeniu din unele ţări UE. *Economie teoretică şi aplicată, XX*(8(585)), 110–122.

Coenen, M., & Kok, R. A. (2014). Workplace flexibility and new product development performance: The role of telework and flexible work schedules. *European Management Journal, 32*(4), 564–576.

Chung, H., & Tijdens, K. (2012). Working time flexibility components and working time regimes in Europe: Using company-level data across 21 countries.

Field, A. (2009). Discovering SPSS using SPSS. London: SAGE publication Ltd; 2009.

Fynes, N., & Storrie, A. (1998). *Families and work in the twenty-first century: Employer benefit from flexible working*. Department of Social and Family Affair.

Jeffrey Hill, E., Grzywacz, J. G., Allen, S., Blanchard, V. L., Matz-Costa, C., Shulkin, S., et al. (2008). Defining and conceptualizing workplace flexibility. *Community, Work and Family, 11*(2), 149–163.

Jones, K., & Jones, E. (2011). Flexible working practices in the UK: Gender and management perspectives. *Journal of Women in Society, 2*, 1–8.

Kossek, E. E., & Michel, J. S. (2011). Flexible work schedules. In S. Zedeck (Ed.), *Handbook of industrial and organizational psychology: Building and developing the organization* (pp. 535–572). Washington, DC: American Psychological Association.

Kossek, E., & Thompson, R. (2015). Workplace flexibility: Integrating employer and employee perspectives to close the research-practice implementation gap. In L. Eby & T. Allen (Eds.), *Oxford handbook of work and family*. New York: Oxford.

Kossek, E. E., & Thompson, R. J. (2016). Workplace flexibility: Integrating employer and employee perspectives to close the research–practice implementation gap. In *The Oxford handbook of work and family*, 255.

Martínez-Sánchez, A., Pérez-Pérez, M., De-Luis-Carnicer, P., & Vela-Jiménez, M. J. (2007). Telework, human resource flexibility and firm performance. *New Technology, Work and Employment, 22*(3), 208–223.

Matos, K., & Galinsky, E. (2014). *2014 national study of employers*. New York: Families and Work Institute.

McNall, L. A., Masuda, A. D., & Nicklin, J. M. (2010). Flexible work arrangements, job satisfaction, and turnover intentions: The mediating role of work-to-family enrichment. *The Journal of Psychology, 144*(1), 61–81. doi:10.1080/00223980903356073.

Noonan, M. C., Estes, S. B., & Glass, J. L. (2007). Do workplace flexibility policies influence time spent in domestic labor? *Journal of Family Issues, 28*(2), 263–288.

Origo, F., & Pagani, L. (2008). Workplace flexibility and job satisfaction: Some evidence from Europe. *International Journal of Manpower, 29*(6), 539–566.

Pitt-Catsouphes, M., & Matz-Costa, C. (2008). The multi-generational workforce: Workplace flexibility and engagement. *Community, Work and Family, 11*(2), 215–229.

***SPSS package version 22

***http://www.bna.com/workplace-flexibility-positive-n17179878803/

***http://www.worklife.emory.edu/workplaceflexibility/quickguides/whatis.html

***http://workplaceflexibility.bc.edu/workFlex

Chapter 10
Compounding in Romania

Angela Vinter

Abstract Albert Einstein used to say that compounding is the "world's eighth wonder." Compounding is a simple investment method and requires only two things: time and reinvesting returns and earnings. This research paper argues the fact that from an economic point of view, compounding in Romania would bring numerous advantages in society, among which stimulating investments, creating jobs, and increasing productivity. It would also greatly reduce the temptation of a shadow economy.

Keywords Profit • Compounding • Fiscal facilities • Economy investments • Accumulation of equity • Stimulating the business environment

In order to determine profit tax exemption corresponding to compounding, the following steps should be taken:

1. The accounting profit corresponding to the trimester/year is calculated, according to the calculation method of the profit tax.
2. The result is compared with the investments from profit made in the trimester/year according to the calculating method of profit tax.
3. The profit tax is calculated for the lowest value of the two, which actually corresponds to the reinvested profit, which will be subtracted from the profit tax that has to be paid.
4. Then the profit tax that needs to be paid will be calculated, which is equal to the profit tax minus the tax on reinvested profit.
5. Allocation to reserves of the profit sum for which the exemption on profit tax was applied, minus the amount related to the legal reserve.

The current tax law offers the private business environment a series of tax breaks. One of these is the tax exemption on profit reinvested in tools (machines, tools, and work stations) acquired after July 1, 2014. The new tax code extended the area of application of the tax exemption for reinvested profit, adding new categories of eli-

A. Vinter (✉)
Emanuel University of Oradea, Oradea, Bihor 410597, Romania
e-mail: angela.vinter@emanuel.ro

S. Văduva et al. (eds.), *Solutions for Business, Culture and Religion in Eastern Europe and Beyond*, DOI 10.1007/978-3-319-63369-5_10

gible assets. *Therefore, starting January 1, 2016*, tax exemption will be applied for reinvested profit in technological equipment, PCs, peripherals, cash registers, control and billing registers, and also software, produced or bought, including on basis of financial leasing contracts, functional, used with the purpose of doing business. It is important to mention that this facility applies to assets considered new and produced and/or acquired until December 31, 2016.

This facility will lead to the increase of investments in economy, given the fact that only 10% of companies make investments at the moment.

A series of authors support this endeavor, of profit tax exemption, also as a measure to eliminate tax evasion, because entrepreneurs will not be as tempted to hide their profit at the end of the year.

The estimations regarding profit rise are, also, positive—32% of the companies are expecting a rise in profitability of over 10% in 2016. This trend will be supported to a great extent through investments, considering that 81% of respondents say that they will increase their investments in 2016, as opposed to 76% that were planning this at the beginning of 2015. These will focus on increasing efficiency, expanding on new market segments and on new markets, as the study *A New Vision of Growth* published by EY Romania shows. These investments will be financed through personal resources and profit reinvestment (46%), followed by bank loans (34%).

The EY study is based on the answers given by 421 top companies, and it analyzes their perception regarding the perspectives of the business environment in Romania in 2016. Twenty-three percent of respondents come from companies with a turnover higher than €50 million, 28% of companies with a turnover between €10 million and 50 million, 35% with a turnover between €1 million and 10 million, and 14% with a turnover under €1 million. The executives responded to EY Romania's survey between January 26 and February 8, 2016.

From an economic standpoint though, reinvesting profit tax would bring advantages to society. First of all, it would stimulate investments; therefore, it would be a measure with the potential of creating jobs and increasing productivity and, thus, real paychecks. Second of all, it would represent a breath of fresh air for companies and would substantially reduce underground economy.

The table below, retrieved from the report of the tax council, shows the profit tax Romanian companies pay overall—3%. Lithuania is the only country out of all the ex-communist ones to have a lower efficiency on this type of profit. The question is if it wouldn't be better for tax profit to be reinvested in order to actually stimulate the economy.

Given the fact that the access to funding for investments is relatively restrictive, especially for SMEs, the measure to not tax reinvested profit has certain economic advantages, by increasing capital endowment but also the level of industrialization, criteria where Romania is way behind in comparison with other European economies. Also, such a fiscal facility brings an extra voluntary financial discipline, through increased efforts to raise profitability and eligibility on a fiscal level.

Numerous countries appeal to various tax facilities regarding profit taxation: Spain, Holland, the USA, Italy, Finland, Latvia, Estonia, Slovenia, and Croatia. For instance, in Spain's case, reducing 10% of the tax for reinvested profit comes with favorable eligibility requirements in case of selling the assets before the law requires. In Holland, for example, capital expenditures and investments in R&D are deducted from the profit tax in a proportion of 54%. In Finland, the package containing fiscal stimulants targets tax exemption of R&D investments, small enterprise stimulants, and a framework of accelerated amortization for capital investments and buildings.

In Romania, tax exemption for reinvested profit is not a fiscal approach that is on the first list of the economic decision table. For instance, in some version, the measure was adopted in 2009, but only until the end of 2010 and more in the letter than its spirit, which considerably held back stimulants and investment efforts that were anticipated.

On the one hand, in compliance with "the letter" of such a fiscal facility, the tax exemption on profit tax took place when technological equipment was produced and/or acquired (art. 19^2 of the Tax Code). On the other hand, "the spirit" of investment stimulant was amputated through certain complementary provisions, meaning determining the book value of the assets by "subtracting from the production and/or acquisition value the sum for which the facility was applied" (ln. 12). Basically, the assets that made the object of the investment were deprived of the additional advantage of being amortized as they were being used. Therefore, the advantages of the fiscal facility were counterbalanced by the impossibility of recovering the investment. In such terms, the measure cannot, de facto, demonstrate its investment potential.

That is why, in order for the fiscal facility to show its fruit, it must ensure the maintenance of the fiscal value of the assets in order to amortize them, so that the investment stimulants be intact. It is important, at the same time, maintaining fiscal stimulants for as long as possible, so that the entrepreneurial calculations not be flawed in terms of "now or never," especially since such a fiscal facility will show its fruit in time, when entrepreneurs will realize the chance they have to capitalize their businesses "through themselves," by revealing profit not just "from the outside," depending on the banking creditworthiness.

Moreover, in the current profitability requirements of the business environment, tax exemption for reinvested profit will not be a burdening measure for the budget, according to preliminary calculations. Even on the short term, the budgetary impact of not taxing reinvested profit could be a positive one.

Evidently, the numbers and calculations on budgetary impact are critical marks. But beyond these, in the foreground of the debate, the essential objective must remain, meaning the decisive stimulation of the business environment, of its investment potential. And the impact will be even more intense if the fiscal facility will be extended to investments in buildings, production facilities, etc.

In the virtue of economic logic and given the current situation, tax exemption for reinvested profit will not harm the state's budget, on the contrary. On the one hand, the entrepreneurs will pursue obtaining profit, and, on the other hand, by increasing technological equipment acquisition, new profit will emerge for other entrepreneurs, production for assets will increase, and new jobs will be created, along with VAT and other taxes related to them.

It's not the national budget that needs to be the engine of economic growth, it's entrepreneurship and capital acquirement too, in a context of economic policies that would consolidate (institutionally and financially) the business environment. In the free, competitive market, capital and profits are the anchors that will pull up, in a durable way, work and paychecks (Cosmin Marinescu, PhD. Professor at ASE Bucharest, Counselor of Minister of Finance on economic policy issues).

Not just obtaining profit is a key challenge for an entrepreneur, but also the way in which this is spent and reinvested. Forwarding resources toward the areas that generate new substantial profits and consolidate the business is no easy job. Things get even more complicated when resources are limited and the company is not on a clear ascendant trend.

In these circumstances, business people must deal with the immense pressure of always finding the correct answer to this question: What percentage of the profit should I reinvest in my business? Which are the priorities toward which the profit should go? There are no universal answers to these questions, but both successful businesspersons and financial consultants argue one thing—profit is the most important financing source for a business. And the advantages of reinvestment are numerous:

- By being an internal financing source, it avoids indebting the company.
- It has reduced costs compared to the external financing means, such as loans from banks or other financial institutions.
- It allows maintaining full control over the business, given that the money coming from another investor may generate vulnerabilities.
- It consolidates company's image—if a business is able to finance its development, it demonstrates its power and success.

But what is the correct approach? Angelo Mendoza, business consultant at RedBiz Inc., a company that helps SMEs solve their cash flow issues, gives some tips regarding the way in which small entrepreneurs can maximize their earnings and lead their business toward success. Although he admits to the fact that a little fun doesn't hurt, Mendoza says that business owners must always put the benefit of their company first.

A good way to resist the temptation of overspending in personal pleasures is that of opening a separate account for profit. The funds coming this way should be used "exclusively for new investments that would target the improvement of products, acquisition of equipment and other facilities, hiring new people, marketing, and advertising campaigns," suggests Mendoza.

Although this consultant's opinion seems restrictive, it may be good to know what a successful businessperson thinks about reckless spending. The Swedish magnate Ingvar Kamprad, founder of international furniture chain IKEA, is even more radical. "Waste of resources is a deadly sin at IKEA," he says. Kamprad also says that everything the company earns is used as a reserve. The fact that these things are not just words is confirmed by the lifestyle lacking excess the founder of the renowned Swedish brand has. At 87 years old, Ingvar Kamprad lives in a modest house, eats at the coffee shop of the store, and shops at the local market.

From an accountant's standpoint, the part of profit that can be invested is determined depending on the balance of the loss and profit bank account, meaning the combined gross accounting profit since the beginning of the year, obtained up until the trimester or the year when the assets are commissioned. Profit tax exemption related to investments made is granted within the limits of the tax profit the company owes for that period of time.

The taxpayers that benefit from this facility have the obligation of preserving into patrimony the technological equipment at least for a period of time equal to half of the economic use, established in compliance with the applicable accounting regulations, but no more than 5 years. For the assets acquired on financial leasing basis, tax exemption is applied by the user.

For the taxpayers that have the obligation of paying a trimestral profit tax, given the situation where investments are made in the precedent trimesters, out of the gross accounting profit accumulated since the beginning of the year, the amount of profit invested before is subtracted.

Tax exemption is either calculated at the end of a trimester or annually, depending on the case. The amount that represents the profit for which the tax exemption was granted, minus the one for which the tax exemption was granted, minus the amount belonging to the legal reserve, is distributed at the end of the financial exercise, with priority on building the reserves until it is concurrent with the accounting profit recorded at the end of the financial exercise. In case that at the end of the financial exercise there is an accounting loss, the profit tax corresponding to reinvested profit won't be calculated, and the taxpayer will not allocate the amount of reinvested profit in the reserves.

For the tangible fixed assets, which are made during multiple consecutive years, the facility is given for the part of investments put into operation in the respective year, when there are situations when the work is finished partially.

From a fiscal amortization point of view, for these tangible assets, the accelerated amortization method cannot be used. When it comes to microenterprises that become income tax payers, in order to apply the facility, the gross accounting profit cumulated from the beginning of the undergoing trimester, invested in the assets provided above, put into operation starting with the trimester when they became payers of profit tax, will be taken into consideration.

In order to determine the exemption for the profit tax corresponding to reinvested profit, the following steps are taken:

1. The accounting profit corresponding to the trimester/year is calculated depending on the method of calculation of the profit tax.
2. It is compared with the investments made from profit in the trimester/year, depending on the method of calculation of the profit tax.
3. Then the profit tax for the lowest value out of the two is calculated, which in fact corresponds to the reinvested profit which will be subtracted out of the profit tax that is to be paid.
4. The profit tax that needs to be paid is calculated, which equals to the profit tax that is to be paid minus the tax on reinvested profit.

5. Allocation into reserves the sum of the profit for which the tax exemption was granted, minus the amount corresponding to the legal reserve.

The fiscal value of those assets is amortized linearly or in a digressive manner, according to art. 28 of the Fiscal Code. For these assets, the taxpayer cannot choose an accelerated amortization.

The reinvested profit started to be on the positive side in 2015, having a positive contribution at the fluxes of foreign direct investment for the first time after the crisis, as shown by Liviu Voinea, vice governor of Romanian National Bank (RNB), when presenting the semester report regarding the financial stability.

For the first time in 8 years, after the crisis began, the reinvested profit becomes positive, meaning it contributed at the total amount of the foreign direct investment. Foreign direct investment is comprised of the actual investment (capital contribution), reinvested profit, and intracompany loan. For 8 years, reinvested profit contributed negatively at the foreign direct investment, meaning money was taken from there.

"In 2015, the money obtained, the profit obtained in Romania was reinvested in Romania. This is a very important evolution," stated Liviu Voinea, in the *Report on the financial stability April 2016* by Romanian National Bank (RNB). The evolution of the reinvested profit signals "an increase of nonresident investors in the local economy," as shown in the report.

Last year, a number of 2365 companies were exempted from paying an amount of 179.4 million RON representing reinvested profit in 2014, according to the information from Ministry of Public Finances, at the request of cursdeguvernare.ro. The exemption on reinvested profit was instated in July 2014 and will be applied until the end of the current year. The Ministry of Finance claims no *decision* was taken regarding keeping this fiscal facility for the future. In 2014, 12.2 billon RON were cashed in at the *consolidated general budget*. The sum represents 5.7% of the total of budgetary income, respectively, 1.8% from the GDP, according to the MPF.

Last year, in 2015, the money cashed in from *profit* tax was of 13.8 billion RON, a 13% increase from 2014. Last year, the amounts collected from *profit* tax exceeded for the first time the ones before the crisis.

Therefore, the *profit* tax collected at the budget in 2015 was 5.9% higher than the one collected in 2008, of approximately 13 billion RON. As a percentage of GDP or in the budgetary incomes, the amounts cashed in from *profit* tax did not reach the level before the crisis, as MPF data shows.

Year	Amount (billion RON)	% of budgetary income	% from GDP
2006	7938.9	7.4	2.4
2007	10,558.9	8.3	2.7
2008	13,045.9	7.9	2.5
2009	11,893.0	7.6	2.4
2010	10,115.1	6.0	2.0
2011	10,309.1	5.7	1.9
2012	10,854.5	5.6	1.9
2013	10,925.7	5.5	1.7

Year	Amount (billion RON)	% of budgetary income	% from GDP
2014	12,237.7	5.7	1.8
2015	13,824.3	5.9	2.0

Source: MPF

I believe that this facility of reinvested profit should be applied for an unlimited period of time, because companies plan their investments ahead and the results regarding economic growth and recovering development will not delay to appear even in the existent global economy.

Bibliography

G.R. 421/2014 to modify and complete Methodologic Norms of application of Law no. 571/2003, regarding the Tax Code.

E.O. no. 19/2014, regarding changing and supplementing Law no. 571/2003, regarding the Tax Code.

Ghid practic complet privind neimpozitarea profitului reinvestit incepand cu 1 iulie 2014 – S&R Accounting Leader, LLC. [Complete Practical Guide regarding Tax Exemption on Reinvested Profit Starting July 1st, 2014 – S&R Accounting Leader, LLC].

Laurentiu Mihai–*Ghidul tau in educatie financiara – 13 regului pe care trebuie sa le respecte un investitor* [Your Guide in Financial Education – 13 Rules an Investor Needs to Follow].

Chapter 11
How Religion Influences Economic Development: A Case on Romania

Urs Hauenstein and Adrian Cioara

Abstract This article intends to study the effect of culture on economy in Romania, observed at the county level. Culture will be defined as common shared values that are derived from religious views, and economy will be understood through macroeconomic indicators such as GDP per capita, unemployment rate, average net wage, and poverty. The objective of this article is to explore whether there is a correlation between the values of the most important religions in Romania and the development of each county. Besides studying the current religious data, the article will present a brief history of Romania showing the major religions that influenced the country's main historical regions.

Keywords Economic development • Religion • Cultural values • Romania

11.1 Introduction

The matter of religion has been largely discussed throughout the ages. Religion has been a major part of the human experience, as people were fascinated by the world around them and dared to find a deeper understanding of what lies at the origin of everything. So man started his journey in the search of Someone that is beyond what is seen. Some called it God, the Aibishter, or the Demiourgos, all of them referring to the One that created the heavens and the earth and should be worshiped in order to obtain his or their—in polytheistic religions' perspective—favor. Many religions have risen suggesting that within their set of beliefs, man can find the Creator, but only one religion has dared to claim that only through its teachings can man find

U. Hauenstein
President of the International Council ICLGEM Solothurn, CH / Honorary Fellow of CGLGR at Leeds Business School, P.O. Box 864, CH-Solothurn, Switzerland, UK
e-mail: urs@hauenstein.london

A. Cioara (✉)
Emanuel University of Oradea, Oradea, Nufarului St. 87 Bihor 410597, Romania
e-mail: adrian.cioara@emanuel.ro

S. Văduva et al. (eds.), *Solutions for Business, Culture and Religion in Eastern Europe and Beyond*, DOI 10.1007/978-3-319-63369-5_11

God—that is, Christianity. Besides claiming that its God is the only true one, as Judaism and Islam do, Christianity claims through its central figure, the Lord Jesus Christ, that: "I [Jesus] am the Way, the Truth, and the Life: no man cometh unto the Father, but by Me."[1] This is an outstanding statement of exclusiveness. Christianity is a religion of exclusivity. Europe is known to be a predominantly Christian continent. From the year 313 AD, when the Edict of Milan was given by the Roman emperor Constantine the Great, Christianity has become accepted in Europe.[2] Since then, Christian teachings have been largely spread within the Roman Empire and, later on, across all Europe through the ministry of monks and crusaders.

The main purpose of this paper is to study the effect of culture on economy in Romania, observed at the county level. Culture is defined here as common shared values that are derived from or were influenced by religious views, while economy is defined by macroeconomic indicators referring to the level of income, unemployment, and poverty. This paper aims to see whether there is a correlation between the values of the most important Christian denominations in Romania and the development of each county. Besides studying the current religious data, the paper will present a brief history of Romania, showing the major religions that influenced the country's main historical regions.

11.2 Why Is Religion That Important?

The former Chief Rabbi of the Commonwealth, Sir Jonathan Sacks, argued in an interview on the future of religion that the twenty-first century will be more religious than the previous one because "the four great institutions of the modern age – science, technology, liberal democratic politics, and the free market economy – cannot answer the three fundamental questions that every reflective human being will ask: *Who am I? Why am I here?* and *How then shall I live?*."[3]

Several reasons strengthen what Rabbi Sacks stated, placing strong emphasis on religion in today's modern studies, especially in the field of development. Firstly, the importance of religion in most of the world challenged the narratives of modernization and secularization.[4] A significant increase has been noticed in the visibility of religion in the public sphere, as part of a new sort of identity politics.[5] The 1979 Iranian revolution, the US evangelical conservatives, and the democratic transitions in Eastern Europe under the auspices of religion are just a few of the examples that show a clear involvement of religion.

Secondly, there has been a dramatic increase in faith-based organizations (FBOs).[6] All around the world, organizations like World Vision, Aga Khan Foundation,

---

[1] John 14:6 (King James Bible).

[2] Frend (1965). The Early Church SPCK, p. 137.

[3] Retrieved on February 2, 2015, from: https://www.youtube.com/watch?v=RV2fDNVb1sc.

[4] Huntington (1998).

[5] Castells (1997) and Casanova (1994).

[6] There is no generally accepted definition of FBOs, but they are often characterized by having one

Christian Aid, Caritas, and others have a major impact by providing services to people especially in the areas of health and education. For example, in sub-Saharan Africa, around 50% of all the health and education services are provided by FBOs, according to a study conducted by the World Bank.[7] Along with their services, these organizations publicly state their values as the example is shown in Fig. 11.1.

Finally, what makes religion so important nowadays for study is related to global security. If in the past half a century, the Western World fought against the communist regimes, today there is a "war on terror."[8] Several terrorist organizations have emerged that claim to fight in the name of religion. One of the newest and fiercest organizations is the so-called Islamic State or Islamic State of Iraq and Syria or just ISIS. It has engaged in a massive genocide in Iraq, Syria, and some African countries in order to fulfill its plans to establish an Islamic caliphate that will be led by sharia (the Islamic religious law). Allied forces from several countries have engaged in combat against this terrorist organization. Unfortunately, terrorism brings religion into discussion under a negative perspective, it being seen as a reason for the existence of these organizations.

Culture represents a system of beliefs which, if accompanied by specific values, become attitudes and define mentalities.[9] Cultures are subjective, varying from one region to another and from one continent to another. They give birth to a sense of identity. The belongingness of an individual to a certain culture determines him to take certain actions that will ensure his security. As values differ, culture cannot be defined from a single perspective. One study has identified 164 definitions of culture.[10] Traditions represent the elements that shape a culture, namely, behavior, attitudes, norms, and values. They can be better understood by seeing them as concentric circles that have in the middle the values—formed by the following three institutions: family, church, and school—then the norms, attitudes, and behavior, as the most external layer.[11]

It can be observed that religion is deeply rooted in the individual's core values. Thus, culture is automatically influenced by the teachings of the predominant religion in that area.

11.3 The Religious Europe

Europe has always been a truly enriched continent, speaking by its cultural dimensions. Religion has always played a very important role in shaping the culture of the European civilizations. Starting from the Ancient Greek and Roman civilization,

---

or more of the following characteristics: affiliation with a religious body, mission statement or activities with explicit reference to religion, and selection of staff based on religion. Clarke and Jennings define a faith-based organization as "any organisation that derives inspiration and guidance for its activities from the teachings and principles of the faith or from a particular interpretation or school of thought within that faith." Clarke and Jennings (2008), p. 6.

[7] James (2009), p. 7.

[8] Holenstein (2005).

[9] Malița (1998), p. 14.

[10] Kreoeber and Kluckhohn (1952).

[11] Salacuse (2003), pp. 15, 22, and 96–109.

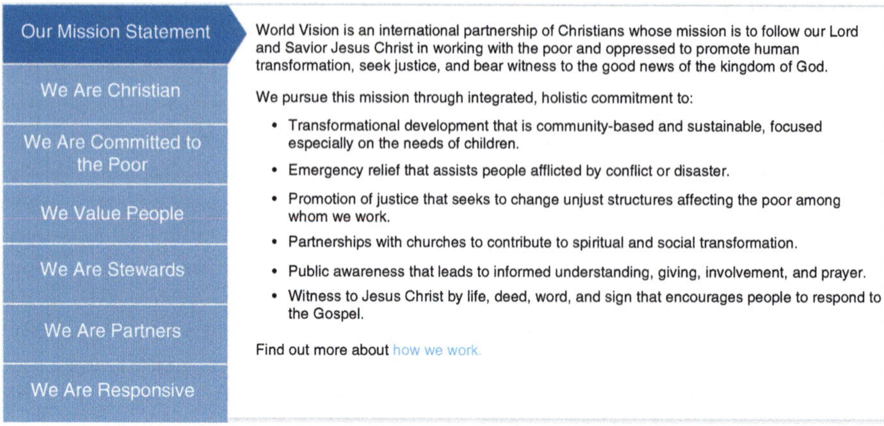

Fig. 11.1 World Vision's Mission. Source: http://www.worldvision.org/about-us/who-we-are

that were strongly anchored in their polytheistic beliefs, heading toward the Middle Ages where Christianity was largely spread and impacted education, arts, the social life, and even, nowadays, religion has a lot to do with the values that people recall. Max Weber demonstrated in his early twentieth-century work, *The Protestant Ethics and the Spirit of Capitalism*, that it was the Protestant values that were at the foundation of developing the capitalist world. This is an accurate example that religion has an enormous impact on economic development, as it also contains issues related to work ethics.

Today, religiosity in Europe is dominated by Christianity, as it has been for centuries. According to the Eurobarometer, 72% of EU citizens identify themselves as *Christians*. The major Christian denominations are Catholic (48%), Protestant (12%), Eastern Orthodox (8%), and other Christians (4%). Also, Europe is the home for 16% nonbelievers/agnostics, 7% atheists, and 2% Muslims, and the number is alarmingly growing in Western Europe, because of high immigration and fertility rates within Muslim communities.[12]

11.4 Macroeconomic Indicators for Romania

For more than 25 years after Romania has turned its side to communism with bloody revolutions that emerged in several parts of the country at the same time, putting an end to the dominance of the Ceausescu regime, the country is still fighting its way to become as competitive as any of the developed European countries. Major

[12] "Discrimination in the EU in 2012," Special Eurobarometer, 383 (European Union: European Commission), 2012: 233, retrieved on August 14, 2013.

developmental changes have been noticed in Romania since 1989, especially around the year 2007 and, afterward, as Romania became a member of the European Union. Today, Romania is developing noticeably, even though it has a long way to reach the quality of life that can be found in Germany, the UK, or other Western countries.

In order to study the development of Romania, four indicators were selected to support the research. The indicators are as follows:

- Gross domestic product (GDP) per capita—the total amount of goods and services produced within the country by local or foreign economic entities per the number of inhabitants
- Unemployment rate—the percentage of inhabitants that are able to work and want a job, but do not have one
- Average net wage—the average amount of money that a person is earning during a month and manages to take home for consumption
- Poverty—the state in which the income of the population is considerably lower (up to 60%) than the national average income

11.5 The Case in Romania

In order to have a better understanding of the data and the assumptions that will be made regarding the impact of religion in Romania's economic development, it is necessary to have an incursion in the country's history. The Romanian people have been formed in what was called the Carpatho-Danubian-Pontus space, namely, the geographic area between the Carpathian Mountains, the Danube River, and the Black Sea (*Pontus Euxinus*, in Latin), as the indigenous population merged with the occupying Roman troops. As the years passed, there were three principalities that corresponded to three major areas: Transylvania (north, northwest, west, center of today's Romania), Walachia (south, southeast of today's Romania), and Moldavia (east, northeast of today's Romania). Each region had its fights to struggle with and was strongly influenced by their neighbors and the populations that migrated. Thus, Moldavia had very strong clashes with the Slavic populations that migrated, which were Greek Orthodox; Walachia was struggling with massive Turkish populations but fought to keep its Christian belief, as Romanians were, as the Slavic, Greek Orthodox. The case for Transylvania was quite different: the principality was occupied shortly after the coming of the Hungarians. Even though the Romanians of Transylvania were Greek Orthodox, after the Christianization of King Stephen I of Hungary, who was Catholic, the clash between these religions was a very strong one. Centuries after, it brought up a new form of religiosity, the Greek Catholicism—this happened many years after—while under the Hungarian dominance, Romanians were given no rights unless they convert to Catholicism, but as they refused, a median solution was found: the creation of Greek Catholicism, which is a mixture between Catholic festivals with Greek Orthodox rituals. But until this, in the twelfth century, two large communities were colonialized in Transylvania. They were the Saxons (*saşi*, a Germanic group of individuals) and the Szeklers (*secui*, a Hungarian group of individuals). These two ethnic groups were about to play a major role in Transylvania because, after the reformation during the life of Martin Luther and Jean Calvin, they were the ones that embraced Protestantism. So, Transylvania became influenced by the Protestant values.[13] Nowadays, if one can take a tour through the major Transylvanian cities, he or she can find that in the center of the town, there lies a Catholic or Protestant Church (Cluj-Napoca, Sibiu, and Oradea are illustrative examples), while if touring through the large cities of Southern and Eastern Romania, the large Greek Orthodox churches prevail. This is a symbol of the impact of religion and church in the local communities and, more important, the specific type of church that has the major influence, as different Christian denominations have different values and different work ethics that have a direct impact on the economic development of a country.

According to the last census (2011), Romania is quite a religious country as 97.51% of its inhabitants declaring themselves as Christians. The main denomination in Romania is Greek Orthodox (85.95%), followed by Protestantism, including neo-Protestantism—Baptist, Pentecostal, and Adventist Church (6.15%)—Catholicism (4.56%), Greek Catholicism (0.84%), and others.[14]

Table 11.1 describes the major Christian religious groups in Romania, according to the last census. The data are sorted by the percentage of Protestant population in each county. The counties with more than 10% of its population being of Protestant faith are all from the historic region of Transylvania. As mentioned before, this is because of the Austro-Hungarian occupation that brought an enormous influence in terms of religion.

Another indicator to be considered is the GDP per capita in each county in Romania.[15] Table 11.2 illustrates the economic situation of every county sorted by the highest value. These data do not show a direct connection between the Protestant population and economic welfare of the county. There are several factors that can influence the GDP per capita, such as geographic position, political status, natural resources, and others.

The same source shows the unemployment rate for each county in Romania. The data are sorted from the lowest unemployment rate to the highest. In the first half, with the lowest unemployment rate, nine of them are in the top Protestant counties. There can be a connection between these data as the Protestant work ethic places an enormous emphasis on a hardworking attitude. The data can be observed in Table 11.3.

Table 11.4 shows the net average wage from the highest to the lowest. It does not indicate a connection between Protestant faith and the level of wages. This could

[13] Scurtu, Cristea, Curculescu, Dinca, and Soare (2007).

[14] [14]Retrieved on April 2, 2015, from http://www.recensamantromania.ro/wp-content/uploads/2012/08/TS8.pdf.

[15] Retrieved on April 2, 2015, from: http://www.gandul.info/financiar/harta-interactiva-a-nivelului-de-trai-din-romania-cat-de-bine-se-traieste-in-judetul-tau-exclusiv-10675712.

Table 11.1 Christian religious groups in each Romanian County sorted by percentage of protestants

County	Christian religious groups in Romania				
	Orthodox	Roman Catholics	Greek Catholics	Protestants	Percentage of protestants
Covasna	43,499	73,739	241	73,848	35.14
Mures	281,113	48,530	11,077	158,331	28.74
Satu Mare	138,032	5340	5726	61,576	27.44
Bihor	321,312	48,350	12,184	156,983	27.28
Salaj	160,776	59,550	24,568	73,136	21.24
Cluj-Napoca	473,096	22,570	23,164	105,216	15.22
Arad	298,252	35,623	4271	57,964	13.46
Bistrita-Nasaud	226,666	3041	5276	35,704	12.47
Harghita	37,670	200,663	516	38,638	12.43
Suceava	532,807	7068	1155	54,816	8.64
Maramures	357,627	22,761	21,836	38,332	8.01
Calarasi	226,230	16,722	1805	21,274	7.20
Hunedoara	337,780	15,367	3620	29,622	7.08
Timis	507,506	54,547	8271	46,144	6.75
Alba	281,888	3369	9294	21,055	6.15
Braila	439,055	17,800	3401	26,015	4.74
Sibiu	333,556	4976	7612	15,364	3.87
Botosani	374,700	581	55	14,741	3.57
Dambovita	482,016	838	74	11,635	2.24
Vrancea	307,260	4373	57	6752	1.98
Galati	486,439	1486	148	10,358	1.93
Ialomita	251,184	162	11	4505	1.64
Prahova	711,117	1807	343	10,957	1.44
Bacau	470,560	96,490	161	8398	1.36
Mehedinti	242,609	1358	71	3575	1.35
Valcea	356,688	5099	50	5084	1.29
Teleorman	348,203	84	16	4861	1.28
Buzau	423,441	492	60	4899	1.09
Gorj	323,217	687	61	3610	1.06
Caras-Severin	278,121	300	43	3154	1.03
Iasi	663,513	35,303	205	7705	1.00
Giurgiu	259,259	383	48	2408	0.86
Constanta	568,094	3912	270	5437	0.79
Ilfov	346,204	6619	214	3010	0.77
Bucuresti	1,587,951	22,149	4016	13,737	0.73
Arges	576,592	812	97	4364	0.71
Neamt	391,722	45,338	138	3324	0.71
Brasov	297,750	813	106	2050	0.64
Dolj	619,298	652	75	3927	0.59
Vaslui	351,851	497	182	1969	0.53
Olt	407,159	173	51	1788	0.41
Tulcea	185,191	350	24	774	0.36

Table 11.4 Monthly net average wage in Romania by County

County	Net average wage
Bucuresti	2,152 lei
Ilfov	1,892 lei
Cluj-Napoca	1,588 lei
Gorj	1,584 lei
Sibiu	1,578 lei
Arges	1,515 lei
Prahova	1,505 lei
Timis	1,504 lei
Constanta	1,448 lei
Brasov	1,418 lei
Iasi	1,411 lei
Dolj	1,381 lei
Arad	1,351 lei
Giurgiu	1,350 lei
Mures	1,330 lei
Galati	1,330 lei
Tulcea	1,327 lei
Mehedinti	1,296 lei
Alba	1,273 lei
Olt	1,260 lei
Buzau	1,257 lei
Valcea	1,248 lei
Salaj	1,247 lei
Ialomita	1,238 lei
Bacau	1,236 lei
Dambovita	1,232 lei
Hunedoara	1,227 lei
Caras-Severin	1,172 lei
Teleorman	1,147 lei
Covasna	1,145 lei
Calarasi	1,140 lei
Satu Mare	1,138 lei
Bihor	1,137 lei
Braila	1,124 lei
Bistrita-Nasaud	1,119 lei
Neamt	1,119 lei
Vrancea	1,098 lei
Maramures	1,091 lei
Vaslui	1,084 lei
Botosani	1,078 lei
Suceava	1,065 lei
Harghita	1,064 lei

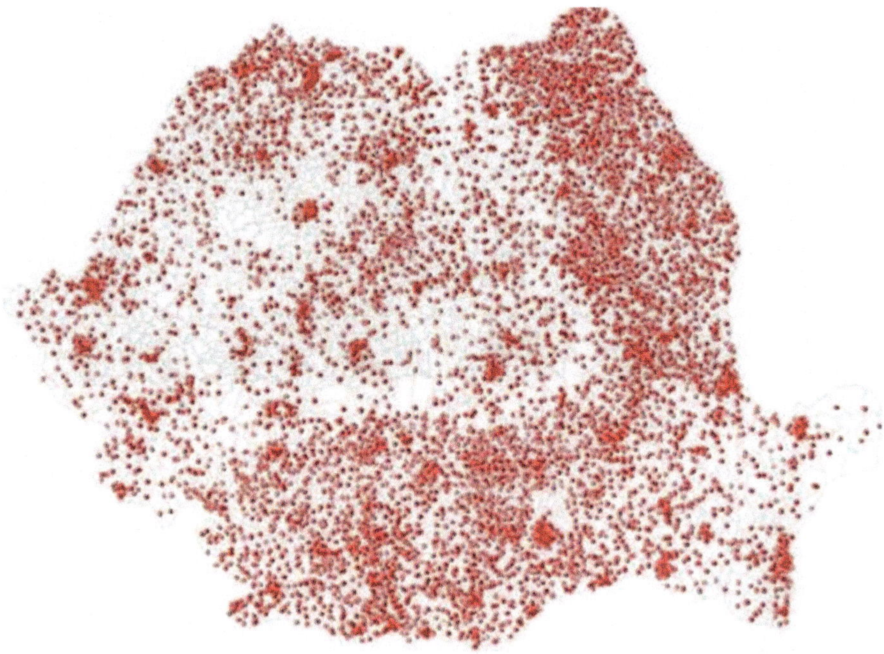

Fig. 11.2 The poverty map of Romania. Source: http://www.capital.ro/harta-saraciei-in-romania-190643.html

be related to the GDP of the county that is influenced by several factors mentioned earlier.

Another set of data relevant is given by the map of poverty in Romania.[16] Each red dot represents 400 people that live below the poverty line. It can be noticed in Fig. 11.2 that the most affected areas are in the east and south of Romania. This indicates that there may be a connection between Protestant faith and poverty. The area with less poor people is the region of Transylvania. There is an explanation for this connection, as Protestants have the virtue of helping others.

After a close analysis of the subject, taking into account the GDP of the country over time as reported by the National Institute of statistics and the percentage of Protestants, we can notice a decreasing trend related to the influence of Protestants on the GDP, especially after 2007 when Romania became part of the European Union. This may be because of the immigration of Romanians toward Western Europe. See below in Fig. 11.3.

[16] Retrieved on April 2, 2015, from http://www.capital.ro/harta-saraciei-in-romania-190643.html.

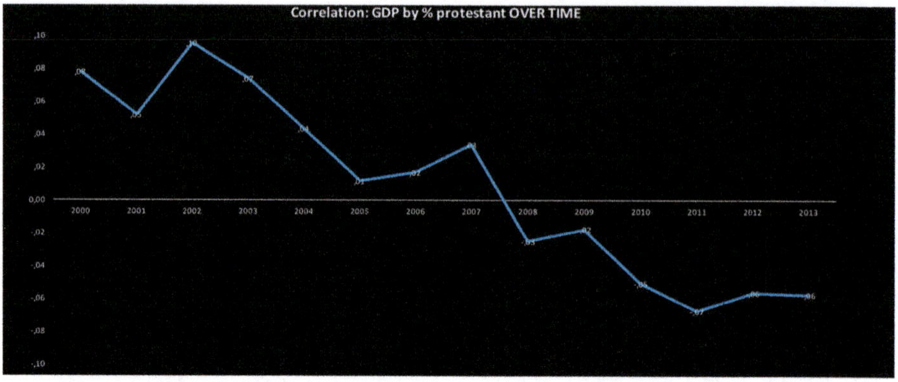

Fig. 11.3 Correlation: GDP by % Protestant over time

11.6 Conclusion

Max Webber's theory argued that the Christian Protestant ethics were at the basis of modern capitalism and economic development. The study on the Romanian context is only partially in concordance with Webber's theory. A slight difference between the well-being of more Protestant counties and of less Protestant ones can be noticed. There are several indicators that do not support Webber's thesis in Romania, but there are a lot of factors to be taken into consideration. This researched has managed to present raw data and show that in terms of poverty eradication and workforce occupation, Protestant counties do better nationwide.

References

Casanova, J. (1994). *Public religions in the modern world*. Chicago: University of Chicago Press.

Castells, M. (1997). *The power of identity*. Cambridge, MA: Blackwell.

Clarke, G., & Jennings, M. (Eds.). (2008). *Development, civil society and faith-based organizations* (p. 6). London: Palgrave Macmillan.

"Discrimination in the EU in 2012", Special Eurobarometer, 383 (European Union: European Commission), 2012: 233, retrieved 14 August 2013.

Frend, W. H. C. (1965). *The early Church SPCK* (p. 137).

Holenstein, A. (2005). *Role and significance of religion and spirituality in development cooperation: A reflection and working paper*. Bern, Switzerland: Swiss Agency for Development and Cooperation.

Huntington, S. P. (1998). *The clash of civilizations and the remaking of world order*. New York: Simon & Schuster.

James, R. (2009). *What is distinctive about FBOs?* (p. 7) (INTRAC Praxis Paper).

John 14:6 (King James Bible)

Kreoeber, A. L., & Kluckhohn, C. (1952). *Culture: A critical review of concepts and definitions*. Papers of the Peabody Museum of American Archaeology and Ethnology (vol. 47). Harvard University.

Maliţa, M. (1998). *Zece mii de culturi, o singură civilizaţie. Spre geomodernitatea secolului XXI*, Bucureşti, Editura Nemira, p. 14.
Retrieved on April 2, 2015. from: http://www.capital.ro/harta-saraciei-in-romania-190643.html
Retrieved on April 2, 2015. from: http://www.gandul.info/financiar/harta-interactiva-a-nivelului-de-trai-din-romania-cat-de-bine-se-traieste-in-judetul-tau-exclusiv-10675712
Retrieved on April 2, 2015. from: http://www.recensamantromania.ro/wp-content/uploads/2012/08/TS8.pdf
Retrieved on February 2, 2015. from: https://www.youtube.com/watch?v=RV2fDNVb1sc
Salacuse, J. W. (2003). *The global negotiator. Making, managing, and mending deals around the world in the twenty-first century* (pp. 15; 22; 96–109). New York: Palgrave Macmillan.
Scurtu, I., Cristea, N., Curculescu, M., Dinca, C., & Soare, C. (2007). *Istorie manual pentru clasa a XII-a*. Bucuresti: Editura Economica.

Chapter 12
The Compatibility Between the Music Expectations of Church Leaders and the Training of Church Musicians in Romania: A Case Study

Lois Vaduva and Simona Popoviciu

Abstract This study aims to research the compatibility between the expectations of Baptist churches in Romania as possible employers of musicians and the training and expectations of music alumni from Emanuel University of Oradea, as possible church music employees. Oftentimes, a disconnection between the music needs of a church and the formal training of a church musician exists, causing a number of issues between the pastor and the church musician. To give insight into this complex issue, a survey was conducted to discover the perspectives of representative Baptist pastors in Romania and also the viewpoints of representative alumni of the music program at Emanuel University of Oradea, Romania.

Keywords Church employment • Music ministry • Church management • Higher education • Employment compatibility

12.1 Introduction

The success of a higher education program is linked to the employment possibilities of its alumni. Unfortunately, the skills that many young people learn in school do not match the skills that the employees need[1]; this creates a crisis in which young people fail to secure a job and institutions are left with vacancies. This crisis is also present in the religious education sector, where Christian universities do not always prepare its alumni for the current needs of the church.

---

[1] http://www3.weforum.org/docs/GAC/2014/WEF_GAC_Employment_MatchingSkillsLabourMarket_Report_214.pdf

https://www.collegetransitions.com/wp-content/uploads/2014/05/robst-relatedness-of-college-major-and-work.pdf.

L. Vaduva (✉) • S. Popoviciu
Emanuel University of Oradea, Oradea, Romania
e-mail: lois.vaduva@emanuel.ro; spopoviciu@gmail.com

S. Văduva et al. (eds.), *Solutions for Business, Culture and Religion in Eastern Europe and Beyond*, DOI 10.1007/978-3-319-63369-5_12

Table 12.1 Regular church attendance

Respondents	Large churches over 100	Medium churches up to 100	Small churches 21 - 30	Affiliate churches up to 20
	31	17	7	2
How many people attend your church on a regular Sunday?				
Less then a 100	8	17	7	2
100 - 250	16	0	0	0
250 - 500	6	0	0	0
Over 500	1	0	0	0

The fourth question highlights the fact that bigger churches are more likely to have a choir than middle, small, or affiliate ones, and as a result, they are more likely to need a church musician. Table 12.2 showcases the information provided by the survey.

In the fifth section, the respondents were asked the following question: "How is music led in your local church?" The results established that out of the total 57 churches included in the survey, 22 churches have a musical group that leads the music, 25 have a singer, 25 churches have their pastor leading the music, and 2 pastors chose not to respond to this question. We mention the fact that in some churches, music is led in more than one way, depending on the church service, some pastors choosing more than one option. The answers to this question indicate the fact that churches have congregational singing during their worship time, and depending on the situation or church, this collective singing is led by a group of musicians, a singer, or even the pastor.

To the sixth question, the respondents were asked to mention the type of instruments used during their church service, this question being included to see if the training of church musicians should include more instrumental classes and instrumental conducting classes but also to find out how developed the music in these churches are. The survey showed that 26 churches use a piano, 42 churches use an organ, 27 churches use guitar, 12 chose "other instruments," and 4 mentioned that they do not have any instruments. Based on this information, the main instruments that need to be included in the education curriculum for a church music program, and that are already taught at Emanuel University, are piano, organ, and guitar.

The next segment investigates the opinion of pastors in regard to the quality of the musical program in their church. To this inquiry, 43.85% answered affirmatively, 24.56% of pastors answered negatively, 26.31% said there is room for improvement, and 5.26% chose not to respond to this question. The results of this point illustrate that even though a significant number of pastors are either not happy or just fairly pleased with the musical quality in their church, 36 of pastors are appreciative of their church music. In this regards, there is an assumption that only the churches that wish to improve their music quality would be more inclined to hire a professional musician.[5]

[5] http://www.reformedworship.org/article/september-1998/care-and-keeping-church-musicians-it-takes-money-and-lot-more-page-1-2.

Table 12.2 The existence of a church choir

Respondents	Large churches over 100	Medium churches up to 100	Small churches 21 - 30	Affiliate churches up to 20
	31	17	7	2
Do you have choir in your church?				
Yes	22	4	0	0
No	9	13	7	2

Regarding the quality of the theological content of the worship time, which was the eighth topic of the questionnaire, 63.15% of respondents replied yes, 3.50% responded no, 22.80% said average, and 10.52% failed to respond. The high number of affirmative answers could be linked to the high percentage of pastors that have theological training, thus giving them more confidence in the analysis of theological content.

The question "Would you be willing to pay a qualified music minister in your church?" was included in the survey to reveal to future possibilities that music alumni have to find employment within a church. We mention the fact that traditionally, musicians in Romanian Baptist churches worked voluntarily, not to burden the churches, which had limited financial possibilities. Oftentimes, a church music leader works in the education system during the week and helps the church on Sundays. In the last years, the paradigm has slowly shifted, churches sometimes employing music alumni to take over the musical responsibilities in the church. The survey offered the following responses:

- From the large churches, 20 pastors would be willing to hire a qualified musician, 9 pastors would not, and 2 pastors did not respond to the question. From the 20 churches that had an affirmative answer, 7 said that they would hire less than part time, 5 said they would hire part time, and 8 would hire full time.
- From the middle-sized churches, 11 answered favorably, 4 had a negative answer, and 2 did not respond to this question. Out of the 11 that answered favorably, 7 would hire less than part time, 3 would hire part time, none would hire full time, and 1 pastor did not answer the question.
- From the small-sized churches, from the total of seven churches, 100% would hire a music minister, four with less than part time, two with part time, and one church would hire full time.
- From the two affiliate churches, one would hire less than part time, and one would not hire due to financial considerations.

The results for this question are encouraging, as a total of 39 pastors are willing to hire a qualified musician, this indicating that there are employment opportunities within churches for alumni of the music program at Emanuel University of Oradea.

The next segment of the survey asked the respondents if they were willing to financially support a music student that is preparing to go into the music ministry. This question was included due to the fact that many potential music students do not have the necessary resources to go to college, and some churches decide to support a talented young person in their congregation to go and get trained. After the completion of their studies, that young person returns home and takes over the music responsibilities. This way, both the church and the student are beneficiaries, the churches getting a return on their investment, through the attainment of a music leader, and the student benefitting from higher education, following the possibility of employment within the church.

The answers to this question are as follows:

- From the large churches, 54.83% said yes, 25.80% said no, and 19.35% did not answer the question.
- From the middle-sized churches, 35.29% said yes, 29.41% said no, and 35.29% did not answer the question.
- From the small-sized churches, 57.14% of the pastors said yes, 28.57% said no, and 14.28% failed to answer the question.
- From the affiliate churches, 100% answered favorably.

Once again, the answers are encouraging, as most of the pastors surveyed answered favorably, this indicating a need for the training and employment of church musicians.

For the *music alumni survey*, we had ten representative music alumni that were chosen from a span of the last 12 academic years. In the first part of the questionnaire, the alumni were asked about the churches that they serve in, the function that they have within the church, and the level of education.

Regarding the size of the church that they work in, the survey indicated that 80% of the music program alumni, with either or both undergraduate and graduate programs, work in large-sized churches and 20% work in middle-sized churches. We notice the fact that none of the surveyed alumni are in small or affiliate churches. As we mentioned before, this is due to the lack of financial possibilities that smaller churches face, in this instance, musicians oftentimes having other jobs to sustain themselves. For example, many of the graduates of the music program at Emanuel University work as volunteers in churches, securing a job as teachers during the week.

At the question regarding the position that the alumni have in their respective churches, we indicate the fact that three alumni occupy more than one function, this influencing the percentages. Also, two of the respondents are fully responsible for the music program in their church, this indicating that they have multiple functions, based on the need of the church. The results are as following:

- Six are conductors.
- Two are both pianists and organists.
- One is both a conductor and a soloist.
- Two are responsible for the entire music program.

As in the pastor survey, the alumni were also asked about the possibility of knowing someone that wishes to study at Emanuel University of Oradea, in the music program. The respondents had the following answers:

- Twenty percent of alumni answered favorably.
- Forty percent said maybe.
- Forty percent said no.

The higher percentage of favorable responses in the alumni survey, by comparison to the pastor survey, is also due to the fact that music leaders in the church are more likely to know about talented young musicians that wish to pursue a musical higher education than pastors.

At the question referring to their academic training, the results were as following:

- Forty percent have undergraduate studies in music.
- Sixty percent have both an undergraduate and master program in music.

This indicates the fact that churches seek qualified and trained musicians to occupy functions in the church.

The following section includes the results of the Likert scale, where we compare the answers of the pastors with those of the alumni to see the difference of perspective regarding the topics that need to be studied for the proper training of a church musician.

The first skills that respondents were asked to rate were the ones pertaining to general music studies. The results are included in Table 12.3.

– For *music knowledge*, we see that most pastors consider this skill as being "important" (26) or "very important" (23), and the music alumni almost all (8) consider it very important.
– Regarding *music theory*, most pastors rated this topic as "important" (26) or "very important" (26), and most music alumni (8) gave the rating "important." Given that general music knowledge and music theory are the foundation of musical training, it is not surprising that both church leaders and church musicians agree to its importance.
– For the *musical arrangements* topic, the opinions differed, 17 pastors and only 2 alumni giving the rating "very important," 21 pastors and 7 alumni consider this skill as "important," and 9 pastors and 1 alumnus gave the rating "somewhat important."
– For *voice* aptitude, most pastors gave the rating "important" (24) or "very important" (13), as did the music alumni, seven considering it "important" and three viewing it as "very important." Eleven pastors gave this skill the rating "somewhat important." Given that most church singing is led by a vocal group, a singer, or the pastor, it is not surprising that most respondents think that it is a necessary aptitude to have.
– The next subject evaluated was *choral conducting*, where just two pastors gave it a "somewhat important" rating, the rest giving it an "important" (21) or a "very important" rating (24). Out of the alumni, seven think that *choral conducting* is "very important," and three consider it "important." From the pastor survey, we

Table 12.3 Importance of music studies

Music Studies	Respondent	Unimportant	Somewhat important	Important	Very important	No answer
General music knowledge	Pastors	0	3	26	23	5
	Alumni	0	1	1	8	0
Music theory	Pastors	0	6	26	16	6
	Alumni	0	0	2	8	0
Musical arrangements	Pastors	1	9	21	17	9
	Alumni	0	1	7	2	0
Voice	Pastors	0	11	24	13	10
	Alumni	0	0	7	3	0
Choral conducting	Pastors	0	2	21	24	10
	Alumni	0	0	3	7	0
Instrumental conducting	Pastors	0	2	18	26	11
	Alumni	0	2	7	1	0
Piano/organ	Pastors	0	0	16	37	4
	Alumni	0	1	3	6	0
Guitar	Pastors	1	6	23	18	9
	Alumni	1	6	3	0	0

know that 26 of the 57 surveyed churches have a choir, so for these churches, choir conducting is a necessary skill. Nonetheless, given the high percentage of affirmative answers, we can deduct that even some of the churches that do not yet have a choir would wish for a qualified musician to know how to form and develop and choir.

- With reference to the *instrumental conducting* ratings, the results were somewhat surprising, as 26 pastors consider this skill "very important," 18 view it as "important," and just 2 gave it a "somewhat important" rating. These results are unexpected, given the relatively few instruments that pastors mentioned that they use during the church service. This may indicate an interest in the development of instrumental church music and the formation of instrumental ensembles within churches. The responses of the alumni also indicated an interest toward instrumental conducting, seven alumni giving it an "important" rating, one alumnus offering a "very important" rating, and two viewing it as just "somewhat important."
- The *piano/organ* skill received a high rating, as most pastors consider it either as "very important" (37) or "important" (16). This was to be expected, as most churches indicated the main accompanying instrument as being either the piano or the organ. The music alumni also found this skill to be important, most indicating that it is "very important" (6) or "important"(3), with just one alumnus rating this ability with "somewhat important." Also, we must take into account a certain degree of subjectivity, as most of the alumni take piano classes, two of the surveyed alumni being pianists/organists within their church.
- The last music subject rated in this section was guitar, which received a lower interest that *piano/organ*. Twenty-three pastors gave it an "important" rating, 18 a "very important" rating, 6 viewed it as "somewhat important," and 1 pastor indicated it as "unimportant." From the alumni representatives, just three gave it an "important" rating, six believe it to be "somewhat important," and one alumnus finds it "unimportant."

Table 12.4 The importance of worship studies

Worship Studies	Respondent	Unimportant	Somewhat important	Important	Very important	No answer
Biblical Worship	Pastors	0	0	26	48	3
	Alumni	0	0	1	9	0
The History of Biblical Worship	Pastors	0	13	27	8	9
	Alumni	0	0	5	5	0
Contemporary Worship Models	Pastors	0	10	28	12	7
	Alumni	0	3	3	4	0
Planning Worship Time	Pastors	0	10	28	12	7
	Alumni	0	1	3	6	0
The Role of Technology in Worship	Pastors	0	0	28	25	4
	Alumni	0	5	3	2	0
Musical Practicum in the Church	Pastors	1	9	32	9	6
	Alumni	0	0	2	8	0

The second set of skills that respondents were asked to rate is in regard to worship studies. The results are presented in Table 12.4.

- The subject of *biblical worship* received the highest ratings, from both pastors and music alumni. Forty-eight of the pastors and 9 of the music alumni gave it a "very important" rating, followed by 26 pastors and 1 alumnus offering an "important" rating. This result indicates the fact that both pastors and music alumni consider that the knowledge of biblical worship is fundamental to the well-being of the church programs.
- *The history of biblical worship* did not offer as much interest, as just 8 pastors consider it "very important," 27 view it as "important," and 13 gave it a "somewhat important" rating. The music alumni are divided in half on this subject, with five considering it as being "very important" and five viewing it as "important."
- The next topic that respondents were asked to rate was *contemporary worship models*, which surprisingly did not receive very high ratings, even though it is still considered important. We would think that this topic is very pertinent to both the church leaders and the music leaders, but the gathered data gives us a different viewpoint. Most pastors (28) gave it "important" rating, followed by "very important" rating, given by 12 pastors, and a "somewhat important" rating offered by 10 pastors. The alumni were divided into three categories: four alumni gave the "very important" rating, followed by three alumni that offered the "important" rating and three alumni which considered this topic as "somewhat important."
- *Planning worship time* received the rating "important" from 28 pastors, just 12 pastors gave it a "very important" rating, and 10 gave it a "somewhat important" rating. More than half of the alumni (6) consider this topic as "very important," followed by six who viewed it as "important," and just one alumnus who gave it a "somewhat important" rating. The fact that percentage wise, more music alumni consider *planning worship time* as very important is due to the fact that in most Romanian churches, the worship time is mostly the responsibility of the music leader.

Table 12.5 Theological studies

Christian Studies	Respondent	Unimportant	Somewhat important	Important	Very important	No answer
Old & New Testament	Pastors	0	0	22	31	4
	Alumni	0	1	4	5	0
Biblical Doctrine	Pastors	0	0	13	39	5
	Alumni	0	0	4	6	0
Missiology/Evangelism	Pastors	0	2	25	27	3
	Alumni	0	3	3	4	0
Spirituality	Pastors	0	0	11	41	5
	Alumni	0	1	3	6	0
Biblical Counseling	Pastors	0	4	21	25	7
	Alumni	0	1	6	3	0

- Half of the surveyed alumni (5) consider that *the role of technology in worship* is just a "somewhat important" issue, the rest viewing it as either "important" (3) or "very important" (2). The reason for this perceived lack of interest is the fact that most Baptist churches in Romania are not large enough to require sophisticated technology during the church service. Many churches do not even have amplification system, as they do not require them. With the modernization and refurbishment of churches, this subject could become of more interest in the near future. The pastors, as "managers" of their churches, have a different point of view than the musicians, this being shown in the results of the survey. Twenty-five pastors consider *the role of technology in worship* as being "very important," and 28 pastors view it as "important."
- The last subject in this section is *musical practicum in the church*. The majority of alumni (8) rate this as "very important" and "important." The pastors also view this as "important" (32), "very important" (9), and just 9 see this as "somewhat important." *Musical practicum in the church* has a high interest, as it is mutually beneficial to pastors and musicians. During the musical practicum, a pastor can beneficiate from having a musician help in the church with minimal financial burden, and the musician has the opportunity to see firsthand all the implications and responsibilities that come with the job.

The final set of skills that were rated by the respondents was the *theological studies*, as musicians also need a good theological foundation in order to be a church musician. The results for this section are presented in Table 12.5.

- The first theological subject rated was *Old and New Testament*. The pastors and the alumni considered this as being either "very important"—31 pastors and 5 alumni—or "important," 22 pastors and 4 alumni, while one music alumnus viewed it as "somewhat important."
- *Biblical doctrines* received a strong "very important" rating from pastors (39) and alumni (5), followed by an "important" rating—13 pastors and 4 music alumni. The emphasis on *biblical doctrines* is not surprising, as most church music that has words must be correct from a theological point of view, and pastors, even more than musicians, are aware of this fact.
- The next subject presented in the survey was *missiology/evangelism*, which received a "very important" rating from 27 pastors and 4 music alumni, an

"important" rating from 25 pastors and 3 music alumni, and a "somewhat important" rating from 2 pastors and 3 music alumni. Many pastors and church musicians consider that music is an effective tool in evangelism, thus explaining the results.

- *Spirituality* received the most "very important" ratings from pastors in this section—41, followed by 11 pastors who gave it an "important" rating. Music alumni also considered this an important subject, with six giving it a "very important" rating, three offering an "important" rating, and just one giving it a "somewhat important" rating.
- The last topic included in the survey was *biblical counseling*, which was considered "very important" by 25 pastors, "important" by 21 pastors, and "somewhat important" by 4 pastors. Most music alumni (6) rated this topic as "important," with three offering the rating "very important" and one alumnus considering it just "somewhat important." There is a consensus between the pastors and musicians in regard to the importance of this subject, as both the pastor and the church musician work with people that have different problems; therefore knowledge in counseling is very helpful.

12.4 Conclusions

The purpose of this research paper was to find out if there is compatibility between what pastors expect from their church music workers and the abilities that music alumni from Emanuel University of Oradea obtain during their training. Two surveys were used to highlight the viewpoints of key Baptist churches and Emanuel University-trained music leaders. Among the important insights presented in the pastor survey is the presence of church musical activity, this being revealed by the presence of church choirs in 26 of churches surveyed. Also, congregational music is used in all the churches surveyed, this being revealed by the question "Who leads congregational singing in your church?" that got various responses, from "a vocal group" to "a singer" and "the pastor." The instruments most used in the surveyed Baptist churches are the piano, organ, and guitar, this proving the importance of the instrumental classes that is part of the music curriculum at Emanuel University of Oradea.

The pastor survey indicated the need and the willingness of most church leaders to hire a qualified musician to take over the musical responsibilities of the church, this being a very important factor in deciding the relevance of the music program. The high demand for church musicians indicates that the music program at Emanuel should continue to cater to the actual needs of the church. Also, an encouraging factor was the eagerness of many pastors to financially support talented young people from their church to complete their studies.

In the survey sections that used the Likert scale, we observe that the opinions of pastors and music alumni are mostly in concordance, from the value that they place on *musical knowledge* and *music theory* to the high rating of *Old and New Testament* and *biblical doctrine*. This indicated the compatibility between the opinions of church leaders and church musicians, which is very important for a healthy working relationship.

One area that would need improvement, based on the survey, is the recruitment efforts of the music program due to the fact that not that many pastors and music alumni being able to identify potential students. This could be solved by a more strategic marketing campaign and by disseminating important information regarding the employment possibilities of the music graduates from Emanuel. Nevertheless, based on the results of this paper, we can conclude that there exists a rapport between the requirement of church leaders and the abilities that the music program of Emanuel University of Oradea provides its students.

References

Faulkner, Q. (2000). *Information vs. formation in the training of Church Musicians*. Faculty Publications: School of Music, University of Nebraska – Lincoln, Paper 18.

Glazner, P. L., & Cimpean, C. (2009). The first Baptist University in Europe: An explanation and case study. *Journal of Christian Higher Education, 8*(5), 422–439.

Graham, G. (2004). The theology of music in church. *Scottish Journal of Theology, 57*(2), 139–145.

Hendricks, A. S. (2012). *A renewed approach to undergraduate worship leader education.* Doctoral thesis, Liberty Theological Seminary, Lynchburg, VA.

Martin Steinmetz, C. (2007). *The work and compensation of the Church Musician* (15th ed.). New York: Boston Chapter, American Guild of Organists.

Routley, E. (1977). Theology for Church Musicians. *Theology Today, 31*(1), 20–28.

Shuter-Dyson, R. (2006). Personality characteristics and the attitude to religion of church musicians. *Psychology of Music, 34*(3), 391–398.

Westermeyer, P. (2015). *Church musicians, reflections of their call, craft, history, and challenges.* Saint Louis, MO: MorningStar Music Publishers.

Printed by Printforce, the Netherlands